Five Facets of a Diamond

A Look at Five Indispensable Elements of Christian Discipleship

by

Dr. Michael B. Brown

With love to Chris & Annie — my new & cherished family,

Michael Brown

PUBLISH AMERICA

PublishAmerica
Baltimore

First printing

ISBN: 1-4241-7720-0
PUBLISHED BY PUBLISHAMERICA, LLLP
www.publishamerica.com
Baltimore

Printed in the United States of America

*This book is dedicated to Adam and Zachary,
Alison and Katharine, whose zest for life
inspires my own.*

– **MBB**

DR. MICHAEL B. BROWN is presently the Senior Minister of Centenary United Methodist Church in Winston Salem, N.C., where he has been since 1998. He is a native of Asheboro, N.C. Married to the former Page Plummer, the Browns have four children: Adam (25), Alison (20), Zachary (19) and Katharine (10).

Dr. Brown graduated from High Point College (1971), Duke University Divinity School (1974) and received his Doctorate of Ministry in Preaching from Drew Theological Seminary (1981). He did clinical pastoral education internships at John Umstead Hospital and Murdoch Hospital, both in Butner, N.C. Prior to his present assignment, he was pastor of Mt. Lebanon Church, Randleman, N.C. (1974-78); Center Church, Welcome, N.C. (1978-82); Stallings Church, Stallings, N.C. (1982-87); Boone Church, Boone, N.C. (1987-92); and Central Church in Asheville, N.C. *1(1992-98),* all United Methodist congregations. In addition to pastoral duties, he has taught Ethics in the College for Seniors at the University of North Carolina-Asheville and New Testament Survey at High Point University.

He has served his denomination as a delegate to General and Jurisdictional conferences (in 1992, 1996 and 2000), as member of The Board of Ordained Ministry (1988-96, serving as Chair of the Preaching Committee) and for eight years as Chair of The Commission on Evangelism and Church Growth (the group which designed *Vision 2000,* which became the model for church renewal endorsed by United Methodism in America). He has served as a member of the Advisory Board for the United Methodist Foundation for Evangelism. He has also written four books and is contributing author to eleven others. In 1995, Dr. Brown was included in C.S.S. Publishing Company's *Great American Preachers* series.

Michael Brown is the recipient of the Circuit Rider Certificate of Merit for Evangelism, the John L. Borchert Award for Christian Communications and the Harry Denman Award for Evangelism. In 1992 Dr. Brown served as one of United Methodism's preachers for *The Protestant Hour* radio program (broadcast on more than 400 radio stations nationally and heard globally via the U.S. Armed Services network). He was a frequent lecturer and preacher at *Vision* 2000 events, having participated in Launch Events and Training Sessions for eleven annual conferences of The United Methodist Church. Also, Dr. Brown has preached on numerous college campuses, including Appalachian State, Duke, Emory, High Point, Wake Forest and Pfeiffer universities and Bennett and Greensboro colleges. He serves or has served on various boards and agencies including The Homiletical Institute of Western NC United Methodist

Church, The Advisory Board of The Florence Crittendon Home, The Advisory Board of Advocacy for the Poor, The Board of Directors for Disciple Bible Outreach Ministries, and on The Trustees of High Point University.

INTRODUCTION

A beautifully cut diamond is always multi-faceted. One holds it in light, and by turning can see the crystalline beauty of each facet. A carefully cut diamond reflects color and light in kaleidoscopic fashion. In fact, diamonds are graded by "brilliance," how light is reflected or refracted when the facets are turned toward a source. Often each facet has its own unique characteristic as it contributes to the brilliance of the whole.

The life of Faith is much like that. It is not one-dimensional. By observing the totality of a Christian, one sees that faith is lived out in a myriad of ways, like the multiple facets of a diamond. All contribute to the whole experience of Christian belief and experience. In this book we will explore five indispensable facets of Faith, five avenues which every believer journeys on the road to wholeness. Even if other areas of Christian living may be considered variables, all of us must deal with

Emotions, Perspective, Calling, Individual Discipleship and Corporate Discipleship.

What follows in the chapters to come will be biblical, often anecdotal and hopefully theologically sound. Study or discussion questions will be provided at the close of each chapter. No exploration of any theme is ever exhaustive or definitive. Rather, as I heard Fred Craddock once suggest about preaching, sermons are intended to help the listeners "chase their own rabbits." It is my desire that the chapters and study questions in this book will help its readers do the same.

Matthew Arnold, in his magnificent poem "Dover Beach," wrote of "the world, which seems to lie before us like a land of dreams, so various, so beautiful, so new...." Read the simple messages here, and dare then to listen to the whisper of a Voice asking you to dream your own dreams, as you inspect the five facets of your own spiritual diamond.

– Michael B. Brown

Table of Contents

FACET ONE: *EMOTIONS*

LIVING AUTHENTICALLY

Read *I John 3: 16-23*

Things are not always what they seem. The story is told about an aged nun who was seriously ill. As she lay in her bed in the convent, younger nuns gathered around her, trying to be of service, and all fearing that she may not survive. One of those young sisters went out to the pasture, took a bucket, milked the cow that the convent owned and then brought the aged nun a glass of milk she had warmed on the stove. But after taking only a sip, the old nun waved it off. The young sister took it back to the kitchen, whereupon she had an idea.

At Christmas, someone had given the convent a bottle of expensive brandy which had never been opened. So, the young woman opened it and poured a healthy portion into the milk, then took it back to the old, sick sister. She put it to her lips, and the sickly nun took a sip. Her eyes brightened a bit. Then she took another sip, whereupon she sat straight up in the bed. She then grabbed the glass and gulped it all down, the color coming back to her cheeks. One of the young sisters said: "It's a miracle. You've been healed. Surely you must have some word of wisdom for us. Please, Sister, share that word." The old nun replied: "All right. Here's the word. Don't ever sell that cow!"

When that nun healed (and sobered up) she would discover that things are not always what they seem. Neither are people. There's a word for that. We call it "hypocrisy." It simply refers to "one who projects a false identity. Not to be what you seem." By those definitions, at either end of the spectrum, neither Mother Theresa nor Al Capone were hypocrites. They both were what they seemed to be. One was authentically good, and the other, authentically evil. But there are others whose lives are not consistent, who seem to be one thing but may be another. Perhaps "hypocritical" is too strong a word to use in describing us. Maybe a better word is "fragmented" or, better still, "inauthentic."

The author of *I John* encouraged infant Christians with the words: *"Little children, let us not love in word or speech, but in deed and truth."* As much as anything else, it was the New Testament's way of calling people to be authentic, to be what we seem. The text refers to the temptation some first-century Christians felt to "talk a good game" about faith without ever playing the game. Apparently those folks went to church, prayed, sang the songs and even publicly referred to themselves as "Christians" (meaning "those who are like Christ"). But in practice, they didn't allow Christ much room to work in their lives. Their faith was more talk than action. In the game of "Show And Tell," their faith was mostly "tell." So John challenged them to *"love (not just) in word or speech, but in deed and truth."* He challenged them to be what they seemed. There is a certain emotional liberation in doing that, in finally confessing "This is what I am," or "This is what I am not, and the world will simply have to deal with it. I will not kill myself trying to live up to everyone else's expectations or down to their temptations. I will simply be who I am!"

In 1992 I came back from a golf course, took my clubs out of the trunk of the car and, after twenty-eight years of playing golf, put them away and haven't used them since. I like golf…as long as I am watching someone play it who knows what they are doing. I particularly enjoy the Senior Tour. I have a blast going to a course and watching Gil Morgan, Hale Irwin or Chi Chi Rodriquez. I will glue myself to a TV to watch Tom Kite and Tom Watson duel their way down the eighteenth fairway. I like golf. I just don't enjoy playing it.

There were things about golfing that I enjoyed. One was the beauty of being outside. But, after twenty-eight years of it, I discovered that I could take walks out of doors a lot cheaper and in less time than if I played eighteen holes. Maybe my favorite thing about golfing was not being near a phone. But, I have also learned that if I am away from the office, and if I simply turn my cell phone off, it accomplishes the same purpose.

Most of all, in twenty-eight years of golfing, my game never improved. I stayed in the woods and the water. I got about as much distance out of a pitching wedge as I did a three wood. I sliced. I hooked. I sliced again in an effort to correct my hook. I broke 90 one time in twenty-eight years. One day I came in all worn out and disgusted at yet another day in the high 90s (both temperature *and* score), and sat down and had a conversation with myself. More or less, I said: "Why do you keep playing this game? Is it because you are having fun?" The answer was "No."

"Is it because you are good at it?" Another "No."

Then came the key question: "Do you play golf simply because other people want you to?" The answer was "Yes."

Friends and church members kept asking me to play, and I kept saying "Yes" because I did not want to disappoint them. So, that day in 1992, I put my clubs away, realizing that whereas I had played golf a long time, in truth, I was never "a golfer." Trying to be something I was not turned out to be frustrating and inauthentic.

One of the greatest voices in Christian theology of the twentieth century preached the party line about human sexuality until shortly before his death, at which time he finally decided to confess that he was, and had always been, homosexual. One of America's leading Christian thinkers, teachers, spiritual mentors and writers for years condemned the very lifestyle that he secretly practiced, almost until the end of his days. When he confessed, he said that the greatest burden all those years had been the knowledge that he was "inauthentic."

A story was reported recently about a small town physician in the Midwest who turned in his credentials because those credentials were fake. He had a fairly large practice in a small town. His patients loved him. Apparently he served them well. But at last his conscience got the better of him, and he confessed that he was not a real doctor after all. He had been a medic in the Army. Doing that, he had learned a bit about the human body and how to treat it. He was a voracious reader and a quick study. He had read volumes and volumes about medicine. He had an uncanny ability to diagnose. His bedside manner was fantastic. A good number of his patients told reporters that they still wanted him to treat them even after they learned he was not really a physician. He probably should have been a doctor. But the fact is, he's not. His credentials were forgeries. At last he learned to love his patients enough to be overcome with (a) fear that from his lack of training he would do something to harm them and (b) guilt that he was a fraud, that he was inauthentic. He grew weary of pretending to be something that he was not.

There is an emotional pain that causes weariness when we try to keep up pretenses, or when we live two lives, or when we say one thing and do another. It is not easy being inauthentic. So, John challenged the church people in our lesson simply to do what they say…to be who they claim…not just to talk the talk, but to walk the walk. *"Little children, let us not love in word or speech, but in deed and truth."*

What does all this say to us—this lesson about being authentic, about not appearing to be one thing when we are, in fact, quite another?

Initially it says that: **It's Not A Bad Thing To Be You**.

Dare to be who and what you are. Don't kill yourself trying to live up to the world's expectations nor down to its temptations. Remember the wise counsel of Emerson: "Envy is ignorance; imitation is suicide." He was saying that we don't know enough about anyone else to be envious. When you try to be like someone else, you forsake doing the one thing that no other person alive can do—which is to be you. For better or worse, you're the only you, and I'm the only me, in the whole world. I am called not to be a phony imitation of someone else but rather to be the best me that there is, to be authentic.

Second, this text says that: **People Learn More By Watching Than By Listening.**

In other words, it is the witness of my life—not just the witness of my words—that ultimately matters most. Let me trot out a couple clichés, which have become that because they are true. The first is simply a statement: "What you do speaks so loudly I can't hear a word you say." The second is a poem:

"I'd rather see a sermon than hear one any day.
I'd rather one should walk with me
than merely point the way."
- Edgar Guest

Particularly this is true with youth. Children are perceptive and intelligent, and they watch us in order to determine whether or not to bother listening to us, whether or not to take seriously what we say. They can tell whether or not we are authentic. *"Little children,"* said John, *"let us not love in word or speech, but in deed and truth."*

Finally, this text says that: **Discipleship Is Not Simply A Matter Of The Heart But Also A Matter Of The Will.**

A recent television documentary was about a man from the Midwest who was engaged to a much younger woman—a very innocent, trusting, moral girl. With the help of a former girlfriend, this man bound his fiancé…tortured her physically and sexually…did it all on videotape…then murdered her…and buried her in the woods. He was arrested, convicted and sent to prison. The reporter asked him how he could live with that memory, and the man answered: "I have no guilt. I belong to Jesus."

Probably none of us will ever experience that much of a gap between what we believe and how we live, but the point is that discipleship is not merely a matter of the heart but also a matter of the will. It is easy to talk about belonging to Jesus; but it is quite another thing to live like we do. It is easy to talk about love or forgiveness in general; but the real test is whether or not I can love or forgive a specific person—especially one who makes it difficult. It is easy to talk about or pray for the poor and hungry; but the real test is whether or not I do anything to offer them food.

To be an authentic, genuine human being does not mean that we are perfect because we are not, nor will we be in this life. Instead, it means that we are real. It means trying to narrow the gap between what we seem to be and what we are, between what we profess and what we practice.

And so, the New Testament tells us: *"Little children,"* be real…be authentic… *"let us not love in word or speech, but in deed and truth."*

Study or Discussion Questions

Ralph Waldo Emerson said: "Envy is ignorance; imitation is suicide."

1. Consider or discuss the psychological implications of that statement.
2. Consider or discuss the biblical/theological implications of that statement.
3. Consider or discuss how that statement applies to you personally.
4. In religion, history or the arts, can you name instances where people sacrificed authenticity in an attempt to be like someone else? What were the results?
5. Name someone whom you consider to be "authentic."

GRAPPLING WITH GUILT

Read *Ephesians 2: 4-10*

Psychologists tell us that guilt is now highest ranking emotion on the stress indicator index. Apparently more people commit suicide from guilt than any other emotion. Psychological surveys also consistently note that that the Number One Fear most people experience is that of speaking in public. That fear ranks even higher than the fear of dying, which means that at the average funeral, most people would rather be the corpse than the preacher! However, a recent survey conducted by a national association of psychological caregivers reported that the second highest of all human fears nowadays is the "fear of being found out." Guilt is the most debilitating of all human emotions.

So, what do we do with this debilitating emotion? How do we handle it, so that in the end it does not handle us?

(1.) **Guilt can be a positive force. There is a difference confessing guilt and feeling guilty.**

I went to a mechanic because my car had a clicking sound under the hood. As the car sped up, the noise would quieten until at highway speed it would go away altogether. Still, a car is not supposed to go "clunk, clunk, clunk" when driving under 65, so I took it in. The mechanic decided to test drive it to hear the noise for himself. He went from zero-100 in about 2/10 of a second. I had never experienced the G-force that astronauts feel until then. Nor had I ever had my entire body pinned to the seat. It was like riding with Dale Earnhardt, Jr. Finally, he stopped and said: "I didn't hear anything." Not trying to be rude, I answered: "Maybe that's because we were going faster than the speed of sound!" In any event, a second mechanic took it for a spin at mere mortal speeds, and he heard the noise. He told me what it was—and how I had to get a second mortgage to repair it—and then he said: "Engine noises are warning signs. Never ignore them. They tell us that something has gone wrong which needs to be made right." Without knowing it, he was speaking psychologically and theologically.

When you feel guilt, listen to it. Examine it. Try to find out what the feeling is telling you. Then do whatever needs to be done. Repair the engine, and move on. That is where many of us imprison ourselves. Feeling guilt, we let it hold us captive. We are like the Prodigal Son when he returned home, beating ourselves up and saying: *"Father, I am no longer worthy to be called your child."* But what did the father do in that story? He threw open his arms, welcomed the boy back home, and said: *"This, my child, is alive again. Let's have a party!"*

Guilt should not be a condemnation of you as a person. Rather, it is a noise telling you that something has gone wrong which needs to be made right. Once you've dealt with it, let it go. As Maurice Boyd preaches so eloquently, there is no reason for you to remember with guilt that which God himself chooses to forget! That's first. If you feel guilt, listen to it. Learn from it. Then let it go, and move on.

(2.) **Second: Christianity is about Grace. Christ is about Grace. The Cross is about Grace.**

You have never done anything wicked enough, low enough or immoral enough that God is not able and willing to forgive it. Your power to sin is not as strong as His power to forgive. *"By grace have you been saved through faith, and this is not your own doing lest anyone should boast. It is a gift from God."*

An old man lived alone in Ireland. He wanted to dig up his potato garden, but it was very hard work. His only son, who would have helped him, was in prison for bank robbery. The old man wrote a letter to his son and mentioned his predicament. Shortly thereafter, he received this reply: "For Heaven's sake, Dad, do not dig up that garden! It's where I hid the money." At 4:00 a.m. the next morning, a team of policemen arrived and dug up the entire garden, but didn't find a penny. Confused, the old man wrote another letter to his son, telling him what had happened and asking him what to do next. His son wrote back: "Dad, now you need to plant your potatoes. Getting the garden dug up for you was the best I could do from here!"

Into our sin and guilt, our sense of self-loathing and failure, God sends Christ—and grace—and open arms—and forgiveness—and fresh starts—and second chances—and he says: "It's the best I can do from here. Now, let go of that guilt. I dug it up. It's gone. It's time for you to plant the potatoes, time for you to build a new life in which that old guilt is no longer around." That is what God himself wants for each of us. The past is past. Let it go. You cannot change a thing you ever did or failed to do. But guilt can cripple you from planting new potatoes, from building a new life in a new way, which is what God desires for you. And that means that guilt is not simply a punishment you inflict upon yourself, it is also an act of defiance against God, refusing to live the life he wants you to live. Let it go.

There is a beautiful old adage that says: "Whoever falls from God's right hand is caught into His left." What an empowering thought, and it's all about God's love and grace.

A story appeared in a national news service about a nine-year-old boy on a baseball lot behind the apartments where he lived in a small town in California. He was playing right field. That's where children play when they can't catch the ball well because fewer balls are hit to right field than to any other place on the diamond. And that is why the other children put him there. His two-year-old sister stood on a kitchen table in their second floor apartment, watching the big kids play and wishing they would let her in the game. She pressed her face against the screen, watching, and the screen began to protrude. Her brother in right field saw what was happening. He yelled to her to get back, but she didn't get back, and the screen popped out. The little girl fell through the air, turning a complete somersault on her way to the ground. Meanwhile, her brother ran to a spot beneath the window, held out his arms, caught her, and carried her back up to the apartment with nothing but a scratch on her forehead to show for it. A reporter heard of the incident, talked to the little boy, printed it in the local paper, and the story was later picked by the Associated Press, which is how I read it. In any event, the reporter asked the child: "Weren't you afraid when your sister fell?" The little boy answered: "I was for a minute, 'cause I ain't too good at catching!" But he did catch her and carried her back up to where she was meant to be.

"Whoever falls from God's right hand is caught into His left." That is the cure for guilt. God loves us not because we deserve it, but because we need it. Even more deeply, God loves us just because we are his. And whenever we fall, in whatever way, He is there to catch us and carry us back up to where we were meant to be. All we have to do is let Him. That is what Paul meant when he said: *"While we were yet sinners, Christ died for us."*

What do we do about guilt? There are only two choices. Either we let it imprison us, debilitate us, and wreck our lives, *or* we listen to it, learn from it, and then hand it over to God and let it go. Grace is God's act of digging the garden. What He asks of us is that we accept the gift, plant the seeds of a new life and let it grow. When we wallow in guilt and self-deprecation, we are literally saying: "My power to sin is stronger than God's power to forgive." Who could be foolish enough to believe that? *"By grace have you been saved through faith, and this is not your own doing lest anyone should boast. It is a gift from God."*

Study or Discussion Questions

(1) Identify three ways in which guilt can be a debilitating emotion:

A

B

C

(2) Identify three ways in which guilt can lead to healing or resolution:

A

B

C

(3) Consider or discuss the meaning of "atonement."

(4) What makes "grace" amazing?

(5) What steps must be taken to receive forgiveness from someone whom we have offended? What steps must be taken to receive forgiveness from God?

BATTLING LONELINESS

Read *Matthew 26: 36-46*

A friend of mine served as chaplain at a V.A. hospital in the mountains of North Carolina. He has an endless supply of stories from his work—some funny, some depressing and some inspiring. I remember one of the latter. A middle aged survivor of Vietnam was a patient in that facility. He had lost both legs in a mine field. He came back to the States to complete his education, earned a doctorate and worked very successfully as a college administrator. But from time to time complications would arise from his amputations—infections and things like that—and he would wind up in the hospital for a few days or even weeks. One day my chaplain friend was talking to the man and said: "You know, I am impressed by all you have accomplished from a wheelchair." The gentleman in the chair replied: "I lost part of my body but I kept all of my soul!"

Perhaps he articulated what is a basic, bottom-line desire in life—the desire to be made whole. The New Testament word for "salvation" is "soteria," which literally translated means "wholeness." Our dream, inherited from our biblical ancestors, is that amid the brokenness of this world—amid the brokenness of our daily lives—somehow we can become whole.

Psychologists tell us that loneliness is epidemic in proportion. Three out of every four American adults claim to feel lonely. They may be married with families, live in crowded neighborhoods, or work in malls surrounded by seas of other people, but still they confess a feeling of isolation and abandonment (as if no one understands and maybe, just maybe, no one even cares). They feel lonely, and that is to feel especially broken.

It is, of course, important to note that there is a profound difference between being lonely and being alone. There were numerous occasions when Jesus chose to be alone. More than once we read that *"He withdrew by himself to a lonely place."* Note that the place was lonely, but Jesus was not. We all know those moments…times when you turn off the ringer on the phone, turn on the answering machine, and lock the door to your room…times when you really hope ESPN, a good book, or Calgon can take you away from the noise, from the conversation, or from the demands of the world. It is not only understandable but also critical that from time to time we find a way to be alone. That, however, is a far cry from being lonely.

Jesus knew about being alone by choice, but he also knew about being lonely even when surrounded by other people. When He preached to a packed house in his hometown of Nazareth and the listeners tried to murder him for what he said, Jesus must have felt desperately lonely. On Palm Sunday Jerusalem's streets were probably crowded with what seemed to be more people than the city had ever known, but Jesus knew how fickle their *"Hosannas"* would prove to be, and how by week's end they would be shouting *"Crucify Him!"* In that moment armed with that knowledge, He must have felt lonely. He knew in The Upper Room that one of the Twelve would betray him and another would deny him. Thus, even as they ate together and the disciples pledged their unfailing love, it is very likely that Jesus felt lonely. In the Garden of Gethsemane where Christ prayed before his arrest, the handwriting was on the wall. He knew what was coming. So, He took his three most trusted friends, Peter, James and John, to be with him. But, as it turned out, they were not essentially "with Him" at all. They were nearby in the garden, but as Jesus prayed *"in agony"* and *"his sweat fell to ground like great drops of blood"* (as he faced the reality of the cross that awaited him) they were not really *with* him. Instead they kept falling asleep. Jesus, though in the presence of others, no doubt felt lonely and, waking them, asked one of the loneliest questions found anywhere in the Bible: *"Could you not watch with me for one hour*?"

"Could you not stay close? Could you not tune in to my life and my pain? Could you not care for me and pray for me and weep with me? Could you not enter into this moment with me to spare me the agony of loneliness? Jesus knew what it was like to be alone. He also knew what was like to be lonely, even when surrounded by other people.

We also know how that feels, don't we?......

To be misunderstood?

Abandoned?

Ignored?

Forgotten?

In pain and no one seems to notice or care?

Frightened with no one to turn to?

Saddened with no shoulders to cry on?

Always letting others lean on you, but there's nobody out there for you to lean on when your weary days come?

At any given moment, over seventy percent of us know exactly how all that feels, even in midst of a crowd.

When Christ's loneliest experiences came (and none were more intense than that Thursday night when he left the Upper Room and went to Gethsemane to prepare himself to face a cross), a handful of decisions on his part seem to have made those experiences bearable.

E.g., Jesus chose to be **WITH PEOPLE**.

He prepared the Passover meal and ate it with his disciples. When He went to Gethsemane, he took those same disciples with him. And when He went deeper into the garden, he asked Peter, James and John to remain near, saying to them, *"Watch with me...and pray."* Jesus knew that cultivating relationships, reaching out to others, and never cutting ourselves off from the crowd is the best antidote we have for loneliness. He chose to be with people.

Years ago I knew a single mom who is a very bright and dear person. She struggled frequently with loneliness. Some nights when her children were with their father, she would arrive at our house around bed time. She had a standing invitation and knew she did not have to call. She just came in and made her way to an empty bedroom. Often she didn't even pause for a conversation. She would simply say: "Tonight I could not face sleeping in that house alone." When the pain of loneliness was overbearing, she chose to be with people.

She made a good point. We can wish for friends, hope for relationships, and long for intimacy, but at some point we have to take action. Do something. Reach out to somebody. Put ourselves in a place where we can meet other people. If friends are "the chocolate chips of life," then at some point we have to be willing to reach into the cookie jar to find them.

When loneliness began to creep in, Jesus chose to be with people. He sought them out, loved them, laughed with them, wept with them, held them close to his heart and thus did not feel so alone.

Second, Jesus chose to be **FOR PEOPLE**.

His life, ministry and journey to the Cross clearly were neither recreational, self-centered nor self-oriented. Jesus lived and died on behalf of others. Here's how He put it: *"The Son of Man came not to be served but to serve, and to give his life as a ransom for many."*

A proven treatment for loneliness is to turn one's energies outward instead of inward…to devote one's self to the service of others…to volunteer at church, to work on a Habitat for Humanity project, to tutor a child or to help at a local service agency. The point is simply that the more we give to others, the more we get back for ourselves.

A certain couple had been married fifty years. The church where they belonged decided to honor them with a reception on their anniversary. During the reception, the pastor asked the couple to step forward and address the crowd. It seems the wife had become rather hard of hearing and unfortunately that day had left her hearing aids at home. Her husband addressed the group of well-wishers and said: "My wife and I have been together fifty years, and she's always been tried and true." His wife leaned over and said: "What did you say?" He repeated it a little more loudly: "I said you have been tried and true." Her face turned red, and she answered: "Well, I'm tired of you, too!"

One of the best antidotes for loneliness is to be "tried and true" in our service to others…to be present for them in their times of need…to be more interested in listening than pontificating…to be more sympathetic than judgmental…more compassionate than preachy…to be someone people know they can count on through thick and thin. When others know that we are there for them, usually they will also be there for us. Furthermore, to lose ourselves in the service of others who hurt is literally to lose ourselves, to lose touch with our loneliness and pain. When we are busy helping others who hurt, we have less time to focus on how much we are hurting ourselves. Jesus chose to be for people.

When loneliness began to creep in, Jesus chose to be with others, for others and, last of all, (III.) He chose to be **WITH GOD.**

"He said to Peter, James and John, 'Remain here, and watch with me.' Then going on a little farther, He fell on his face and prayed." Jesus understood that though we may feel lonely, in truth we are never alone - that God is ever near, ever loving, ever accessible to anyone who calls his name in prayer.

An aging widow who lives with her dog deep in the beautiful Appalachian Mountains talked with me about living alone. I asked: "How do you combat the loneliness?" She answered: "Sometimes at night when I sit in the house, I read the Bible. Often when I work in the garden, I pray. And in those moments, I can feel the embrace of unseen arms."

"Then going on a little farther, Jesus fell on his face and prayed." He knew that though we may sometimes feel lonely, in truth we are never alone. Through prayer we feel the embrace of unseen arms.

Loneliness comes to everyone from time to time. It truly is unavoidable. But, there are measures we can take to address it and keep on living. When loneliness crept in for Jesus, he chose to be: (1) WITH PEOPLE...(2) FOR PEOPLE...and (3) WITH GOD.

Study or Discussion Questions

(1) What is the difference between being "alone" and being "lonely?"

(2) Are there ways you can identify loneliness in another person?

(3) How can a person of faith respond to the lonelienss of other individuals? (Be specific.)

(4) What lessons can we learn from our own experiences of loneliness?

(5) Are there specific things we can do to resolve our own sense of loneliness? If "yes," list them.

A BALM FOR GRIEF

Read *I Corinthians 15: 12-19, 51-57*

I am neither a nihilist nor even a pessimist. I am, however, a realist. And as such, I have a theory about life. Here it is: *"Life is not the last five minutes of the movie."* For the first hour and twenty-five minutes of a movie, there are problems and foul-ups galore, but in the last five minutes somehow Tom Hanks and Meg Ryan always get together. The real world is rarely so neat or happily-ever-after.

Until recently I suspect I was the only person left on the planet who had not seen *On Golden Pond.* Now, we have all seen it. I cannot imagine why I waited so long to rent the video. In the last five minutes of that movie, Henry Fonda is helping Katherine Hepburn, who plays his wife, move a box of her mother's china. Fonda has just turned eighty and has health problems. Suddenly he drops the box, grips his chest and falls on the porch.

Hepburn races for his nitroglycerin pills. Then she begs God not to take her husband. "You don't want him, God," she pleads. "He's just an old fool!" Immediately the Hollywood miracle occurs. Both Fonda and Hepburn realize that he just strained a muscle lifting the box of china. He's fine. He gets up, dusts himself off, and the two of them walk hand-in-hand to stand on the pier and watch the sun glimmer on Golden Pond. Such were the last five minutes of a wonderful movie.

However, in reality, both Fonda and Hepburn are gone now. In the end, there was no script writer who could change that for them. Life—real life—is rarely like the last five minutes of a movie.

Down deep, we all know that. Just look at the titles of some of the nation's recent best-selling books: *Stiff (The Curious Lives Of Cadavers)*...*Plague*...*Pox*...*Toxic Psychiatry*...and my favorite, Elizabeth Wurtzel's book *Prozac Nation* (which, I am told, is being made into a movie). We know that life is anything but a Hollywood fairy tale.

Paul understood that, too. He provided a laundry list of problems he had experienced in his own life: being ship-wrecked...adrift at sea...without food...falsely accused and imprisoned...and three times flogged almost to death. When it came down to the last five minutes of his movie, there was no magical deliverance from suffering. Instead, he was convicted of the crime of preaching Christ and was sentenced to die. Paul knew that life is not always fair.

There is a delightful book of cartoons in print. All appeared in *The New Yorker* magazine and all are about dogs. On the back cover is a picture of two dogs sitting in a back yard, talking. One dog says to the other: "I bit a person once. It tastes just like chicken." The book is entitled *Scotch And Toilet Water*. What a great title! It states it right there on the cover that life is not the last five minutes of a happy movie. It is instead a mixture of good and bad...joy and sorrow...love and loss...*Scotch And Toilet Water*.

Life, says *The New Yorker* and the Bible, is not always fair.

Good people get sick.

Young people become addicts.

Babies go hungry, while a derelict dies of malnutrition in a skid row tenement with $90,000 hidden away in his mattress.

There are *"wars and rumors of wars."*

Children are abused.

The elderly are neglected.

In the land of Jesus' birth, Christian children are afraid to walk to school.

In the city of Jesus' birth, residents are virtually imprisoned within a wall imposed upon them.

Good people suffer from everything from arthritis to AIDS.

And at last, there is the matter of death, the cruelest of all life's tragedies. You stand beside a grave and weep bitter tears, you watch loved ones with broken hearts, you say "goodbye" to someone who is absolutely irreplaceable, you struggle to remember the sound of a voice as it called your name, and there is no script-writer around who can change it all and write a happy ending. In those bitter moments, how does one find the strength to keep on keeping on?

Paul asked the same question. *"If we have hope in this life only,"* he wrote...if this life is all there is, if ultimately our lives are nothing more than momentary blips on some cosmic screen, if it truly is *"ashes to ashes and dust to dust"* and nothing more...*"then we of all people are most to be pitied!"*

But, Paul continued, this life is not all there is. *"Behold, I tell you a mystery...We shall all be changed, in a moment, in the twinkling of an eye...."*

Certainly Paul used those words to describe the literal change from physical death to life eternal, but the words are also pertinent to those of us who grieve. There you are, dampened by tears...feeling empty and numb...wondering how the world can just go on as if nothing happened...when suddenly, unexpectedly, *"in the twinkling of an eye,"* something happens to bring comfort.

It may be a card or a phone call. It may be the memory of a hymn or scripture verse from your childhood. It may be a photograph or the memory of something a loved one said or did. Or, it may be an unexpected act of kindness from a friend or a stranger.

The week after my father died, a family in our church was gracious enough to let me use their place at the beach to rest, relax, reflect and re-group. One day I went to lunch in Wilmington, North Carolina. I was standing alone in a buffet line, waiting to reach the food, head hung down, having a hard time dealing with the memories of a dad who would so much have enjoyed being there. Suddenly there was a little voice, like an angel's, which maybe she was. "Hi, my name is Alicia. I'm three. What's your name?" There stood a beautiful three-year-old African American child with her hair in braids, smiling up at me. She walked over without being invited, hugged my leg and then extended her arms for me to pick her up. Her mom nodded that it was okay, so I did. Little Alicia softly nestled her head on my shoulder. I stood there and hugged her, remembering when I used to hold my boys that way and how good it felt and even remembering being held in my own dad's arms.

Her mom, almost apologetic, said, "Sometimes she's too friendly. Alicia, you need to get down." I mouthed the words so the child could not hear but her mom could: "My father died last week. I needed this hug." So her mom waited and smiled as her three-year-old child surprised a grieving stranger with the gift of love. I believe God hugged me through Alicia.

Most have been there. Sometimes *"in a moment, in the twinkling of an eye,"* something unexpected happens in the midst of your grief, and you feel God's hug.

But, there is even more that brings us comfort. A faith, a hope, that life at the end is not merely extinguished. For *"if we have hope in this life only, then we of all people are most to be pitied!"* Paul believed and taught that the Resurrection of Christ meant that all God's children can count on that same resurrection.

"For the trumpet will sound, and the dead will be raised incorruptible...(so that) *death is swallowed up in victory...O Death, where is your sting? O Death, where is your victory?...Thanks be to God, who has given us the victory through our Lord Jesus Christ!"*

The book *A Man Called Peter* was Catherine Marshall's biography of her husband, the famous Presbyterian minister and chaplain to the U.S. Senate. Remembering his unexpected death, she wrote of how Peter Marshall was lying on a stretcher, dying, and through his pain he whispered these final words to his wife: "Darling, I'll see you in the morning." In the dark months following, she asserted it was his unshakeable faith in a new morning where life goes on forever that gave her the strength to survive his death. And later, it was the memory of the Faith he had always preached—especially the faith in a God of comfort who will not let us grieve alone—that helped her heal.

And so, to all who have suffered the loss of loved ones, to family members who have wept bitter tears, there remains a word of comfort straight from the heart of the Christian faith: (1) Life does not end at the funeral. Instead, for those whom we have loved and lost, life that is endless begins there. Jesus said so himself: *"And I, if I be lifted up, will draw all others unto myself."* (2) Our loved ones, in their living and loving, left us lessons for our own lives. When we remember those lessons, our loved ones stay alive through us. And, (3) the God who has received their spirits to be with him in Heaven will also send his Spirit to be with us in our grief.

My father used to quote William Cullen Bryant's poem, *"To A Waterfowl."* How beautifully the poet articulated Christian faith in the face of grief:

> Thou'rt gone! The abyss of heaven
> Hath swallowed up thy form; yet on my heart
> Deeply hath sunk the lesson thou has given,
> And shall not soon depart.
> He who, from zone to zone,

Guides through the boundless sky their certain flight,
In the long way that I must tread alone
Will lead my steps aright.

Study or Discussion Questions

Psychologists tell us there are five stages of grief:
– Shock (This can't be true!)
– Denial (This doesn't seem real.)
– Anger (This is not fair!)
– Guilt (If only I had…)
– Resolution and Recovery (Discovering a "new normal.")

Consider or discuss how the Christian Faith is experienced or expressed in each of those five stages.

FACET TWO: *PERSPECTIVE*

ATTITUDE MAKES A DIFFERENCE

Read *Philippians 2: 1-18*

A friend sent me an internet report of a man named Andrew Wanewenter who some time ago retired from the Milwaukee, Wisconsin, Police Department. Most of the time when someone retires it is not national news. That day it was news because Detective Wanewenter was eighty-six years old and still working eight hours a day. In fact, according to his department, he was still solving crimes. When asked the secret to his longevity, success and happiness, Detective Wanewenter answered in one sentence: "It's all about attitude!"

Paul understood that and wrote to the Philippian Christians saying so. He knew they lived with hard times, and even harder times were coming. As already noted, for the most part the Christians in Philippi were rather poor. They frequently struggled to keep their heads above water. Also, not far off on the horizon, Paul could see the approaching Roman persecution of the infant Christian Church. Those people lived in hard times, and even harder times were on the way.

Additionally, Paul wrote to them from a prison cell under the sentence of death. If anyone knew about hard times, Paul did. So they listened when the evangelist challenged them to maintain a strong and faithful attitude, even in the face of suffering.

The apostle trotted out for the people of Philippi a list of positive attitudes that can make all the difference between a life of joy or a life of despondency: *"Encouragement"* - *"Comfort"* - *"Love"* - *"Fellowship"* - *"Spirit"* - *"Tenderness"* - *"Compassion"* - *"Joy."* Human natures tells us that there is only so much emotional space in any person, and we choose how to fill it. We can fill it with positive or negative things, but there is only so much space. Paul suggested qualities to the Philippians that he felt could fill their inner space positively and therefore could effectively combat depression and despair.

He offered two very specific pieces of advice about maintaining a healthy perspective. First, *"Each of you should look not only to your own interests, but also to the interests of others."* Almost everyone can remember a time when they felt blue, lonely or cheated by life but for unexpected reasons at that very moment were thrown into helping somebody else. Maybe your neighbor had an accident, or it was your day to volunteer at the hospital. After a while of focusing on the needs of other people, you did not feel so discouraged or blue anymore. Paul was a good psychologist. He knew the more we help our neighbors, the better we feel ourselves. So he wrote: *"Each of you should look not only to your own interests, but also to the interests of others."*

Paul was also a good theologian. His second piece of advice was: *"Have that attitude within you which was also in Christ Jesus...who took on the nature of a servant...and humbled himself...and took up a Cross"* on our behalf. Jesus saw the world through God's eyes. So he wrote to the *Philippians* and said: *"Have that attitude within you which was also in Christ Jesus."*

Attitude makes a difference in virtually every endeavor. When two teams take the field for the Super Bowl or World Series, one of those teams will have an edge in attitude. One will have prepared better mentally; they will feel more confident, almost unbeatable. And that team will go home with the trophy. Each team is made up of stellar athletes, All Americans, guys with the size of a lion and the speed of a gazelle. But one team will want it more or believe more in themselves. And they will win.

Red O'Quinn was an All American end who played football at Wake Forest University years ago. He went on to play for the Washington Redskins. My dad got to know him some years after O'Quinn had retired. He told Dad something I found interesting. "There were days as a Redskin when we took the field, and I knew we were going to win," he said. "No one could defeat us that day. There were other Sundays when we didn't have the winning attitude, and I knew we would lose. The game is so mental," said O'Quinn, "that usually the outcome was decided before we even left the locker room."

How many times have you heard someone say, "I knew I shouldn't have married him when I did it?"

"I knew I shouldn't have tried to start that business."

"I knew from the outset I couldn't make it through med school."

And their prophecies were self-fulfilling. Paul understood that. So he labored to get the Philippians to approach life with a positive mind-set, the kind that gives you at least a fighting chance at success. *"Have that attitude within you which was also in Christ Jesus."*

There is a verse in *Proverbs* that says the very thing Paul was saying to the *Philippians*: *"As people think in their hearts, so they are."* It is the Bible's way of saying that attitude does make a difference.

British psychiatrist, Dr. J.A. Hadfield, wrote a book entitled *The Psychology of Power*. In it, he told of asking three people to submit themselves to a test about the effect of mental suggestion on their strength. It was measured by having them grip a dynamometer. They were to grip it with all their strength under three different sets of conditions. First he tested them under normal conditions. The average grip was 101 pounds. Then he tested them after he had hypnotized them and told them that they were very weak. Their average grip this time was only 29 pounds. In the third test Dr. Hadfield told them under hypnosis that they were unusually strong. The average grip jumped to 142 pounds. His conclusion was: That which we believe about ourselves we frequently become.

Suppose, for example, you want to be professionally successful. Can you envision yourself that way? Can you see the steps it takes to get from here to there? If so, you can make the journey.

I read recently that a TV show featuring a psychic was cancelled. He probably is a very nice man. Maybe he is a psychic, who knows? But when his TV show was cancelled, he said: "I was surprised by what the network did. I didn't see it coming." If you are a psychic, shouldn't you be able to see it coming?

What do you "see coming" in your professional life? Or your personal life? Romantically? Relationally? Academically? An old adage says: "If you can conceive it, you can achieve it!" And though that may not work in every case, it is still good advice. As Paul told the *Philippians*, "Attitude Makes A Difference!" Believe the best about yourself and your neighbors, and that is what you will usually find. Look for the worst, and it will be there.

Norman Cousins wrote the best-selling book, *The Anatomy of an Illness: As Perceived by the Patient*. In it he wrote of being hospitalized with a rare, crippling disease. When it was diagnosed as incurable, Cousins checked himself out of the hospital. He knew that negative emotions can have a negative effect on the body, so he assumed perhaps the opposite was also true. Thus, he went out and borrowed a movie projector. Then he bought old Marx Brothers movies and copies of the "Candid Camera" TV show. He watched them over and over. He discovered that every ten minutes of laughter produced two hours of pain-free sleep. In time, with enough laughter and positive emotions, his disease went into remission.

That is not to say that every illness can be cured by laughing, but it is to say that attitude makes a difference in most of life's endeavors. The mind is a powerful thing. And it is remarkable what can happen when, to quote Paul, we *"have that attitude within you which was also in Christ Jesus."* What happens, for example, when we make up our mind that?:

I *can* forgive that person, and I will!
I *can* find a way to help that situation, and I will!
I *can* learn to love that man or woman, and I will!
I *can* make a difference in my church or my community, and I will!

Paul shared a couple pieces of powerful advice with his friends in Philippi, friends who were facing tough times and who needed to find inner strength.

(1) Paul reminded them that the more they focused on helping others, the less they would worry and fret about themselves. One of the great antidotes for depression is to lose ourselves in making life good for somebody else. How did he put it? *"Each of you should look not only to your own interests, but also to the interests of others."*

(2) And, Paul reminded them that for better or worse, usually we find in life just about what we are looking for. As Detective Wanewenter put it, "It's all about attitude." So, Paul wrote: *"Have that attitude within you which was also in Christ Jesus."*

And so we hang onto an attitude of peace even in a world of war,

And an attitude of kindness even in the face of hatred,
And an attitude of grace even when others are hostile,
And an attitude of joy even when our neighbors are cynical,
And an attitude of faith even when society is, at best, agnostic,
And an attitude of hope even if we are tempted to give up.

Many years ago, Claire Booth Luce said: "There are no hopeless situations in life; there are only people who have grown hopeless about them." That sounds much like Paul when he wrote to the *Philippians*—Paul who knew first-hand and told others that sometimes the only difference between winning and losing or even surviving in life is attitude. *"Have that attitude within you which was also in Christ Jesus."*

Study or Discussion Questions

(1) What factors contribute to (a) bad attitudes and (b) good attitudes?

(2) What control can we exercise over any of the answers listed in question #1?

(3) How does one's faith affect his/her attitude about daily issues in life? (Not about broad scale philosophy or theology, but rather about the day-to-day events and occurences in a person's life.)

(4) Identify a biblical character who suffered from a poor outlook. Why did you pick that particular person?

(5) Identify a biblical character who displayed a positive attitude about life. Why did you pick that person?

YOU CAN DO ALL THINGS

Read *Philippians 4: 10-13*

A defense attorney phoned his client, saying: "I have some good news, some bad news, and some more bad news." The client said: "Give me the bad news first." The attorney answered: "The blood tests are back." He paused, and his client said: "Well? What's the other bad news?" The lawyer answered: "It matches your DNA." The client gasped and said: "Then what could possibly be any good news?" The attorney answered: "Your cholesterol is down to 140."

There are times when a person is hard pressed to find any good news in a situation. Surely it must have been that way for Paul—writing from a prison cell—sentenced to die—loving and missing his people in Philippi—and knowing the hard times they would soon face. But even amid all that, Paul said: *"I rejoice greatly in the Lord, for I have learned to be content in all circumstances...I can do all things through Christ, who strengthens me."*

Could any of us honestly say that? If we confuse the words "content" and "happy," then no one would make that statement.

How can you be happy with the economy in and out of recession and jobs being lost by the tens of thousands every year?

How can you be happy with a national terrorism alert at the high orange level?

How can you be happy when you read about Israel and Palestine, Iraq and Iran, India and Pakistan, North and South Korea, Northern Ireland, Ethiopia or Darfur?

How can you be happy if you are one of the fifty percent of American couples currently going through a divorce?

Or one of the seventy million Americans battling depression?

Or one of the forty-one million people suffering from HIV/AIDS?

How can you be happy with new reports every day of car bombings and random murders in Iraq?

Or if you are a spouse or parent watching your loved one ship out for The Persian Gulf?

Or if you observe the ongoing violence between Israel and Hezbollah?

Fill in your own blank of personal heartache or sorrow. Whatever cross you are carrying, it is not always possible to be happy *"in all circumstances!"*

However, Paul says it is possible to be *"content."* The Greek word he used meant "at peace." Paul was not "happy" about his imprisonment—nor about the poverty of his friends in Philippi—nor about the coming persecution they would have to suffer—but he was *"at peace"* because he knew the Hands that held him.

An arresting picture appeared of a Louisiana family in a shelter following a Hurricane Katrina. Along with hundreds of others who had been evacuated, that family was spending the night in a high school gym. Winds were howling outside the building. Water was destroying everything in its path only a few blocks away. The threat of personal loss was high; the threat of personal injury was real. And yet, there were two children (small, pre-school children, probably about three and five, a brother and a sister) sound asleep. How could they sleep through all the hell that raged around them? One was cuddled in his mother's arms, and the other lay quietly on her daddy's lap. It was a picture with theological power. The children were not existentially "happy" in treacherous circumstances, but they were "at peace" because they knew the hands that held them.

No matter what life threw his way, said Paul, *"I have learned to be content in all circumstances."* Not "happy," but "at peace." He knew (whether full or hungry, rich or poor, applauded or persecuted, in freedom or in a Roman prison cell) that God's hands held him tightly. So Paul was at peace. Thus did he tell the Philippians to surrender themselves—their lives, their fears, their dreams—to those same loving hands.

Then Paul wrote to his friends in Philippi one of the most famous statements ever written: *"I can do all things through Christ, who strengthens me."*

One wonders if the *Philippians* were convinced. For that matter, are we? However hard I try, and however deep my faith, the truth is I cannot leap tall buildings in a single bound. I cannot do all things.

I cannot sing like Pavarotti.

I cannot paint like Bob Timberlake.

I cannot hit a baseball like Barry Bonds.

I cannot write a check like Bill Gates. (Actually I could write it—it's just that you couldn't use it for anything.)

Let me read through a copy of *Gray's Anatomy*, I still cannot perform surgery.

Let me watch all the instruction tapes in the world, I still cannot play golf like Tiger Woods.

I cannot make all people like me or even like one another.

It really does not matter how deep my faith, there are things I simply cannot do. But perhaps that is not what Paul was actually saying. Rather, he may simply have been saying: "I can do what I have to do. I can do what I am called to do. I can do what lies in front of me and cannot be avoided, however overwhelming or frightening. I can do more than I thought I could do, if Jesus gives me the strength."

A daily devotional article told of a family doing yard work. They were working on a flower garden in front of the house, and the garden was to be surrounded by large stones—not boulders, not unmanageable things, but large enough to give you a good-sized backache if you aren't careful. The five-year-old son in the family watched his daddy roll those rocks, one by one, into place around the garden. Finally, he said, "Daddy, can I do it? Can I roll one of the rocks?"

Grinning slightly, his father said, "Here son, you can try with this one." Before the little boy started trying to push the rock, his dad offered another piece of advice. "Son, I'm sure you can do it if you use all your strength."

The little guy started. He had seen his daddy do it, and he was sure he could do it, too. But the rock was heavy, the ground was damp, and the stone would not budge no matter how much he huffed, puffed and pushed. Finally, almost worn out, the little boy said: "You were wrong, Daddy. I can't move it."

His dad smiled and said, "No, son. You didn't do what I told you. You didn't use all your strength."

The child said, "What do you mean, Daddy?" and his father answered, "You didn't ask me to help."

Sooner or later we all have heavy rocks to move in our lives (at work, at home, in school, in church) and, on our own, we cannot budge them. But we can face whatever life throws our way if we use *all* our strength, which means asking for the help of a heavenly Parent. Whatever you are facing in life, that Parent stands nearby always waiting to lend a hand in facing whatever has to be faced, in doing whatever has to be done. On our own, the tasks and challenges of life are sometimes absolutely overwhelming. But, as people of Faith, we are not "on our own." Bishop C. E. Linney of the A.M.E. Church used to say: "The task before us is never as great as the Power behind us." Or, as Paul put it (enduring life in a prison cell): *"I can do all things through Christ who strengthens me."* So can we all.

Study or Discussion Questions

(1) What three things do you like best about yourself?

A

B

C

(2) How can each of those attributes be a tool for Christian discipleship?

(3) Consider or discuss the meaning of "self-fulfilling prophecies." How do they contribute to/detract from a sense of satisfaction or wholeness in life?

(4) What is the difference between self-confidence and arrogance?

(5) Identify your primary source of strength in life? Defend your answer.

BEYOND ASKING "WHY?"

Read *Ecclesiastes 3: 1-8*

Early in his junior year at college, my older son Adam was walking across campus at the University of North Carolina-Asheville with his friends Karen, Stephen and Russell. They were on their way back to the dorm—back to watch some TV—back to get ready for Tuesday morning classes. As they walked on that cool, starlit mountain evening, they talked and laughed. My son said, "We were having a great time." Russell, his friend, was just a freshman. It was his first year at a university. One can imagine how excited he was as he adjusted to campus life. On his own for the first time. Growing up. Wondering about his major and meeting the right girl and planning his future. As the four of them walked toward the dorm, suddenly without warning Russell fell to his knees and then on his face. He was unconscious when he hit the ground. By the time the ambulance arrived he had quit breathing. Adam saw them put his friend in the back of the ambulance. He saw them using paddles on him. And he heard a little while later that Russell—just a kid, only eighteen—had died.

To those who are in high school or beginning college, I apologize for what I am about to write. But to a parent, college freshmen are just children. It really hasn't been that long since you held our hands when you crossed the streets, or since we changed your diapers, or rocked you to sleep in our arms. Eighteen is young. It sounds younger every day. At eighteen you are just getting started. You're standing in the narthex of life. You haven't even gotten into the main rooms yet. Laughing, talking and walking in the moonlight with friends, at eighteen a person is much, much too young drop to the ground and die.

John Ritter died when he was only fifty-four. That's young. And he hadn't even been sick. He burst onto the scene in *Three's Company*. Then there were some movies. After that was the loss of a marriage and a bit of a dry spell in his career. But suddenly he was again happily married, a loving father, and the star of a hit sitcom on ABC. Life had resurrected for John Ritter. Then on a Thursday night, while filming his show, he simply fell over. His aorta just came apart, they say. Emergency surgery could not save him. His life had come back together just in time for it to end.

The local paper in my town carried two stories the same morning. One was about the deaths of three young sisters in a limousine on their way back from a concert, hit by a drunken driver. The other was about a young high school football player who was accidentally shot. In each story, family and friends, through tears, asked, "Why?"

How do we cope with the death of a young soldier in Iraq who was simply standing in line at a school hoping to purchase a cola? Or a young Iraqi man on his way to a food market, mistakenly identified as a terrorist?

And what about the innocent victims of a nationally troubled economy, good hard-working people in every community whose opportunity to work has been taken away?

Sometimes life just doesn't seem fair. And however much you ponder or pray about it, it's still troubling. That's what made Rabbi Harold Kushner's book so popular a few years ago. It was called *When Bad Things Happen To Good People*. He wrote it following the death of his teenaged son to the rare illness *progeria*, also known as "rapid aging." His little boy literally died of old age in front of Kushner's eyes, and there was not a thing he could do to stop it. As a person of faith, he could not understand why that tragedy would occur. And so he asked his question: "Why?" Why do these horrible things happen to people who do their best and live their best and love their best and do not deserve such pain? When he posed his question the book became a best-seller, which obviously meant that millions of others are asking the same thing.

It is not a new question. As far back as *Job*, religious thinkers have been asking why a good God would allow such horrible things to occur to people. The traditional responses are familiar:

– Orthodoxy says you cannot know pleasure without

the option for pain; otherwise, we are mere puppets in God's playhouse.

– The Old Testament pre-Job view was that suffering is a punishment for sin (which some people still preach).

– The deists (including the founding fathers of our country, people like Washington and Jefferson) believed that God made us, but after that we're on our own and…good luck!

– Calvinists thought that some people are simply predestined to suffer.

– Christian Scientists taught that evil doesn't actually exist, so suffering is just an illusion.

There are all sorts of projected answers to the question that Job and others like Rabbi Kushner have asked: Why do bad things happen to good people?

Scholars call the author of *Ecclesiastes* "Koheleth" (which is a Hebrew word that just means "the preacher"). Koheleth was very much a different guy from Job. He did not ask "Why?" Instead, he looked at life from a realist's viewpoint. He said that bad things simply happen. So do good things. It's the way the world is made. It may not be the way we would like it, but it's the way it is.

"To everything there is a season, and a time for every purpose under heaven: A time to be born, and a time to die; A time to plant, and a time to pluck what is planted; A time to kill, and a time to heal; A time to break down, and a time to build up; A time to weep, and a time to laugh; A time to mourn, and a time to dance; A time to cast away stones, and a time to gather stones together; A time to embrace, and a time to refrain from embracing; A time to gain, and a time to lose; A time to keep, and a time to throw away; A time to tear, and a time to sew; A

time to keep silence, and a time to speak; A time to love, and a time to hate; A time of war, and a time of peace."

There is a natural rhythm to that—breathing in and breathing out. Birth and death...reaping and sowing...weeping and laughing...war and peace. Koheleth said: That's the way the world is made. Good and bad alongside each other. Mountains and valleys. Sunrise and sunset. It may not be the way we would like it, but it's the way it is. As I sometimes tell people: "This isn't Heaven yet."

Obviously none of us desires hardship or suffering. Three members of a local church were talking to each other at the barber shop. One of them said, "When you die and your friends view you in the casket, what do you want them to say?" Arthur answered, "I want them to say, Arthur was a good church worker, a good husband, and a good family man." Eugene said, "I want them to say, Eugene was a wonderful teacher, had a great sense of humor, and made a difference in the church and the community." Finally, Tom said, "I want them to say, Look! He's moving!"

Most of us are like Tom, and understandably so. We do not want suffering to come. But the truth is, want it or not, it still comes. And like Job, we wonder why.

To be perfectly honest, even if we could answer the question "why," what difference would it make? It would not in any way take away sadness or pain. It would not in any way change the outcome of things.

A lovely young woman was murdered during her senior year at Duke. I served as minister to her parents. The girl's mother was not concerned with securing justice by having the murderer (her daughter's roommate) put to death. She even plead with the court not to impose capital punishment. I remember that mother said: "The courts will do what the courts will do, but in the end I will not have my daughter returned to me." She had moved beyond the question "Why?"

That is how Koheleth dealt with the question of evil and suffering…not by asking "Why?," but rather by asking, "What now?" Evil simply happens in this world. Jesus himself said so: *"The poor will be with you always."*

"There will be wars and rumors of wars." So, the issue is not so much learning why those things happen but rather learning how to cope when they do—what to take from moments of defeat that will help us attain future victories—how to use our suffering as equipment to love and heal others who suffer, too.

If one were to ask for a show of hands in most churches, what percentage might go up if the minister said:

Who here has ever lost a parent?

How about a spouse?

Or a child?

Or a job?

Or a marriage?

Or some measure of your health?

Who here has ever taken medication for depression?

Or had serious surgery?

Or almost lost your life in an accident?

Or in a war?

Readers who answered "Yes" to one or more of those questions are not alone. Almost every adult in or outside any church would do so. No matter how bad life may seem at the moment, we are not the only person who ever carried a cross. We are not the only person who ever suffered. And if we knew "why" any of those tragedies in one's life occurred, would it change them even a single iota? The point is what we have done with our tragedies…or, what we have allowed them to do to us.

Chester Mayfield was a minor league baseball player in the mid-1950s. He was certain to have a great future in the major leagues. He could hit like Mickey Mantle and run like Jackie Robinson. But, just before he was to be called up, he had a hunting accident and lost his left arm—and with it, his dreams of being a big leaguer. Many of us (maybe most of us) would have lost hope under similar circumstances. But Chester Mayfield went on to spend his life joyfully—productively—working with handicapped children and making their lives bright. When asked how he managed to deal with his tragedy, Chester said: "God gave me the strength to survive, and then he asked me to pass that strength along to the children."

Why did Chester Mayfield lose his arm? Who knows? But if we did know, would it have made the arm grow back? The point is that in his tragedy he found two things: the loving, healing presence of God *and* the wisdom to use his suffering as a tool to help other people who suffer.

"*To everything there is a season,*" wrote the author of *Ecclesiastes, "and a time for every purpose under heaven. A time to be born, and a time to die…A time to weep, and a time to laugh; A time to mourn, and a time to dance…A time of war, and a time of peace."*

Good happens. So does evil. It's simply how life works. When pain and suffering arrive, we can surrender to sadness. Lots of people who exist as emotional zombies have done just that. But, we also have the option to lean on a Higher Power and learn the lessons only suffering can teach. The old adage goes: "Suffering either makes us bitter, or it makes us better." Chester Mayfield chose the latter and years later said, "God gave me the strength to survive, and then he asked me to pass that strength along."

Study or Discussion Questions

(1) Reflect upon an event of significant human suffering.

(A) How did you feel when you read about or experienced it?

(B) What questions sprang to mind?

(C) What actions did you take?

(2) When that event occurred, was your understanding of God (a) troubling in light of the tragedy or (b) comforting to you?

(3) Reflect upon an instance of personal loss or suffering.

(A) How did you feel when you read about or experienced it?

(B) What questions sprang to mind?

(C) What actions did you take?

(4) When that event occurred, was your understanding of God (a) troubling in light of the tragedy or (b) comforting to you?

(5) Reflect upon the personal and theological meanings expressed in this poem:

I walked a mile with gladness.
She chattered all the way,
But left me none the wiser
For all she had to say.

I walked a mile with sorrow,
And ne'er a word said she,
But oh, the things I learned from her
When sorrow walked with me.

FIND YOUR FOCUS

Read *Matthew 13: 24-30*

Clichés on this topic abound. How about....

Some see the glass half empty; others, half full.

Or, *Two men looked out from prison bars.*
One saw the mud, the other, stars.

Or, *A dog's nose sniffing down, smells the dirt.*
A dog's nose sniffing up, gets warmed by the sun.

There must be a million different old adages about building and maintaining a healthy sense of perspective. But, just because something is clichéd doesn't mean that it's simplistic or should be dismissed. Wisdom literature is simply "proverbs that stood the test of time." And proverbs are simply clichés that people embraced and passed along. The simple fact is that usually a cliché becomes a cliché because it is true. Thus, perhaps there is depth, wisdom and even Godliness in that little phrase we have heard all our lives: *"Some see the glass half empty; others, half full."*

Jesus seemed to think that is a significant lesson for living life with meaning and joy. That's why He told the parable about the weeds and the wheat. Some servants came to the owner of a field, almost frantic. *"Sir,"* they said, *"someone has come and sowed weeds in your wheat field. My goodness! What shall we do? Do you want us to mow the field and kill all those nasty weeds?"* And the owner, looking out the same window at the same field, answered: *"No. Lest in gathering the weeds, you destroy the wheat as well. Let them both grow together till the harvest…then the weeds will be gathered into bundles and burned, but the wheat will be gathered into my barn."* What a wonderful study in contrasts. Some look at a field and focus on the problems and pitfalls while others look at the same piece of land and see the beauty of wheat and the potential of a harvest.

To be sure, sometimes the particulars of life in the moment make it difficult to focus on the good, the bright, and the happy.

A six-year-old boy was making his first airline flight. His normal hyperactivity was multiplied about ten times over by the excitement of being on a plane. So, he was all over the place…running up and down the aisle, making countless trips to the bathroom, asking a thousand questions, bothering the other passengers, knocking on the door the cockpit. Finally, racing up the aisle, he bumped into a flight attendant and sent her sprawling.

He had managed to get on her last nerve. So, she picked herself up, dusted herself off, looked at the child and said in the sweetest voice she could muster: "Son, why don't you go outside and play."

There are moments when it's difficult if not impossible to see the silver lining. And yet if we look closely enough, it's almost always there.

Long ago I came across this proverb on needle-point plaque in a gift store: "There are basically two kinds of people in life. Some are so focused on the negative that they weep when counting their gold. Others, even in the midst of misfortune, find reasons to sing." It is simply another way of stating what Jesus taught in his parable: Every life is a mixture of good and bad, happy and sad, wheat and weeds. It is up to us to determine whether we will focus on one or the other, whether we will weep or sing. The simple fact is, we usually find in life whatever we're looking for, good or bad. No matter how many weeds there are in your field, you can always find wheat if you are willing to look for it.

A respected Baptist minister from the deep South went through a desperate season some years ago. His mother, almost 80, died one night in a house fire. They found her two feet from a window, deceased from smoke inhalation. Less than a month afterward, he came home from his church one evening and found a note on the kitchen table—a note from his wife, telling him that she had been in love with someone else for a long time and had left town to be with her lover. In less than thirty days, he lost his mother and his spouse as well as his sense of self-esteem and hope and even, understandably, a little bit of his faith. How wonderful it would be to write that the very next week someone made a brilliant remark that turned him around, or a bright light descended from the skies and whispered encouragement. But none of that happened. Instead, he went through what he described as "a year submerged in hell." It was painful. It was depressing. And he struggled simply to survive from one day to the next. However, he did survive and in time built a new and wonderful life. This is what he said about that experience: "I am a better pastor now than I ever was before I suffered those losses. In times past, people would come to my office with their broken lives, and I would treat them with impatient sympathy, nodding my head and glancing at my watch. But now they come, and I treat them with empathy. I understand what it means to hurt, and somehow they seem to know that I know." That is not how any of us would choose to learn life's lessons or become caring and empathetic to others. But it is an illustration of how life works—that no matter how dark the clouds, there are always silver linings if we look for them. No matter how obvious the weeds, there is always wheat in the field if we choose to see it.

Some will say, "That's just rose-colored glasses. That's just Pollyana. Out there in the real world, sometimes there are tragedies too dark and desperate to be redeemed. Some fields have no wheat." Christian faith does not believe that. Instead, the faith that has sustained believers for two thousand years proclaims that no matter how tragic a given situation may be, life's evil forces are never stronger than God. He is always able to help us find blessings even in the bad times.

In 1996, nine-year-old Amber Hagerman disappeared from her Arlington, Texas, neighborhood while riding her bicycle. An eyewitness was able to give some details of the car involved, but no system was in place to get that information to local residents quickly. Amber's body was found four days later. Hoping to prevent such a tragedy from ever happening again, residents contacted area radio stations and suggested that special alerts be broadcast in abduction cases in the future. The Association of Radio Managers in the Dallas/Fort Worth area worked with local law enforcement to develop an emergency broadcast plan. Thus, the *Amber Alert* was born. In 2005, for example, there were thirty-four Amber Alerts in the state of California alone, and every single child was safely returned to their home. Did any of that bring Amber Hagerman back to her parents? Did any of that wipe away their grief or sense of loss? No. But out of the tragedy was born a blessing for countless other families, and safety and hope for countless other children. Were there weeds in the Hagerman field? Undeniably, yes. But also, in time, there was wheat.

Fortunately, most of us never have to endure a tragedy of that scope. But the simple fact is, we all have our burdens to bear. There are weeds in every field. But God can move into our sorrow, given the chance, and give us the power to survive and to learn valuable lessons that only heartache can teach.

And then there is this. Not only does every field have weeds, it also usually has a lot more wheat than we sometimes confess. Put another way, life is usually much better and much brighter than we give it credit for being.

Jack Canfield, one of the co-creators of *Chicken Soup For The Soul*, said in a television interview that he got his positive outlook from his grandfather who loved to say:

"I believe that the world is plotting to do me good!" What a wonderful way to live! "I believe that the world is plotting to do me good!" That sort of perspective brings joy because we usually find what we're looking for. If we believe there is goodness, hope, happiness and love out there, then that is ordinarily what we will find.

Joni Eareckson Tada, confined to a wheelchair as a quadriplegic, often tells us her audiences that "every morning is a new gift. Every bird at my window brings music. Every phone call from a friend brings hope. Every touch from my husband brings love. Each new day gives me new chances for laughter and hugs and relationships and entertainment and letting my mind run even though my body can't walk. Do not feel sorry for me," she says to her listeners, "for every morning I feel the warmth of God's smile, and every night I sleep cradled in his love." Perspective! She has a million reasons to be unhappy but has chosen instead to focus on the million other reasons she has to give thanks.

Ultimately we all have to decide what will dominate us—despair or delight. And when you come to the end of the journey, wouldn't it be tragic to think that you wasted all those years focusing on the weeds of life, when there was so much lovely wheat right there in your garden?

Study or Discussion Questions

(1) Identify three personal strengths/skills that you possess.

(2) How can you employ those gifts for the benefit of church or world?

(3) Identify three ministries that your church does well.

(4) How can those ministries enhance the life of your community?

(5) If studied in a group, go round the circle with each person saying to the one at his/her right hand: "The thing I like most about you is..."

(6) If read alone, spend a moment meditating on the phrase: "I know God loves me because..."

FACET THREE:
CALLING

CALLED BY MERCY

Read *Ephesians 2: 1-9*

Kyrie Eleison (*"Lord, Have Mercy!"*) is one of the historic prayers of the Church, often associated with the season of Lent, which can be a dark and brooding time of the year. It is a season of penitence and prayer, a time for facing up to our personal sins and failures. But right in the middle of Lent stands the Cross, a symbol of the inexhaustible love of Jesus Christ and the lengths to which that love would go to rescue us from our guilt. So, the primary theme of Lent, as well as the whole Christian year, is always *Mercy*—how the reality of our sin comes face-to-face with the reality of His love.

Often when we hear the word "mercy" we think immediately of the other word "forgiveness" (which a poet called "the scent of the violet on the heel that crushed it"). The truth is, however, that whereas forgiveness is merciful, mercy is more than mere forgiveness. It is instead "acceptance"—to accept, affirm and even love the other person, just as they are, and sometimes in spite of what they are.

An acquaintance in the ministry told me of a man in one of his early churches who intentionally hurt him. He told lies about my friend and sought to undermine his ministry at that church just because they disagreed about some little issue in an obscure committee. For several years that church member continually and consistently made life hellish for my friend. Likewise, throughout his ministry at that church and for years afterward, my friend carried a burden of deep, dark resentment against that man, a resentment that bordered on hatred. Years later, the two of them bumped into one another. Here's how the minister told the story:

"Something inside me told me the time had come. So I walked across the room and extended my hand to my old enemy, unsure of whether or not he would take it. He did. And for a long time that day we stood and talked and laughed and shared stories. Neither of us ever said, 'I'm sorry,' but we both knew. The anger was over. And I walked away with the greatest sense of peace. I hope he felt it, too. Jesus was right," the clergyman said. "Resentment is just too heavy a burden to carry around."

I asked, "So, how's the other guy now? Over the years since that encounter, what has your friendship with him been like?"

The minister answered: "Oh, I haven't seen or spoken to him since."

Did those two men forgive one another? In all likelihood they did. But, did they take the next step to accept and embrace one another? Obviously not.

Forgiveness appears to be something that was turned inward. They each found inner peace by letting go of the burden of resentment which is just too heavy and uncomfortable to bear. As such, forgiveness is something we do for ourselves. We lay down our own inner burden. But "mercy" is something we do solely for the other person.

The author of *Ephesians* said that God not only forgives our sins, but he goes the next step. He accepts and embraces us as his children. In fact, He does that even while we are still sinners. Here's how the lesson put it:

"But God, who is rich in mercy, out of the great love with which he loved us, even when we were immersed in our sins, made us alive together with Christ...By grace you have been saved."

In other words, God goes beyond forgiveness to mercy. He accepts and embraces us as his children, even when we don't deserve it.

There is no better illustration of that principle than Jesus' story of The Prodigal Son. In that story, the father represents God, and the prodigal represents most of the rest of us. The son rejected his father's home and values. He ran away and lived a miserable, sinful, self-indulgent life. But finally, the story says, *"he came to himself."* He realized what a disaster he had made of things. So, he went back to his dad, head hanging and hat-in-hand, and said: *"I am no longer worthy to be a part of your family. But, would you be willing to treat me as one of your hired servants?"* Can we truly hear his request? He was simply asking for forgiveness. But what did the father do? He embraced his son and shouted out to his servants: *"Cook the fatted calf. Put a ring on my boy's finger and shoes on his feet. Let's have a party. For this, my son, was dead, and is alive again. He was lost, but now I've got him back!"*

"This, my son...!" The father didn't stop with forgiveness. He extended mercy. He accepted, affirmed and loved the boy as part of the family even in spite of himself.

One day recently I had two wonderful meals. Admittedly, for me any meal with a large quantity of food and without liver or pickled beets is wonderful. Even so, that day it was the conversation more than the food that made the meals great. I had lunch in Chapel Hill, NC, with author and professor Tim Tyson. That night, I had dinner in Winston-Salem, NC, with John Killinger, the renown preacher/scholar and his wife, Anne. An interesting thing occurred. Both at lunch and at dinner I heard the same phrase used *verbatim*. Tim said it, and later that evening John said it. The words were these: "From time to time in life, no matter who you are or how hard you try, we all stand in need of mercy."

That has been the theme song of my life. At age twelve I sensed a Call into ministry. The sky didn't open, nor did I hear a Voice as did Paul on the road to Damascus. But still, at age twelve I knew. I knew why I was alive. I knew why God put me here. I knew my purpose as much as I knew my own name. God wanted me to be a preacher. But, I also knew something else, and I've known it ever since: God has strange taste in who he calls to do sacred work. Me, of all people! Totally human, often sinful. Just a plain old flesh-and-blood human being with more Achilles heels than I have feet. Why on earth would God call me? After all, I thought preachers were practically perfect, and I was just the opposite. So, why did God call me?

Across all those growing up years…and those high school years…and those college years…and all the years since when I have let him down over and over again, why did God keep calling me to do his work and preach his Word? The answer? Mercy. At some point, *"God, who is rich in mercy, out of the great love with which he loved us, even when we were immersed in our sins"* decided to embrace me, affirm me and choose me to do his work.

Why does God love, accept and use an imperfect person like me? For the same reason that He loved, accepted and used drunks like Lot and Noah…concubines like Esther…thieves like Jacob…crooked tax collectors like Zaccheus…prostitutes like the woman in Simon's house who anointed Jesus with costly perfume…murderers like David…and accomplices to murder like Paul. For the same reason that after Simon Peter denied even knowing him and left him to die, Jesus sought Peter out and called him not once but three times: *"Feed My sheep."*

Why is God interested in people like them, and me, and you? The answer is "Mercy."

On June 1, 2005, Percy Arrowsmith, 105 years old, and his 100-year-old bride, Florence, celebrated their 80th anniversary. Percy died two weeks later. They met at their church in Hereford, England. He sang in the choir, and she was a Sunday School teacher. According to *The Guinness Book Of World Records,* until his death they held the record for the longest marriage. At their anniversary party, they were asked what was the secret of staying together, and staying in love, for eighty years. Among the things they listed was this: They said that every night before turning out the lights, they would look at each other and acknowledge what had happened that day, good or bad. If there had been a problem, they would be honest about how irritated or angry either of them had become at the other. But then they would each repeat these words: "What happened today isn't half as big as the love I feel for you." Then they would kiss goodnight, turn out the lights and drift off to sleep in one another's arms. For eighty years, whenever the need was there, they practiced mercy…and mercy kept their love and their relationship alive.

When we turn to God with guilt or sorrow, when we cry out *"Kryie eleison"* ("Lord, have mercy!"), he always answers: "The sin that you committed is not half as big as the love I feel for you." And so He keeps on choosing us to be his children and cradling us within the shelter of his loving arms.

Study or Discussion Questions

(1) Identify three gifts of mercy Christians are called upon to offer their neighbors.

A

B

C

(2) How does one practice mercy to those who are resistant?

(3) Identify three mercy ministries Christian churches may offer to the world.

(4) Contrast the statement of John Wesley, "The world is my parish" to the attitude of some church people, "This church is my world."

(5) Is Grace ever conditional? Defend your answer biblically and theologically.

COUNTING ON CHRIST

Read *Hebrews 13: 8-9*

For the most part, I admire politicians on both sides of the aisle. Washington, Jefferson, Lincoln, Franklin Roosevelt and Dwight Eisenhower were politicians, just like Churchill and DeGaulle and even Ghandi. America and the rest of the world are forever in their debt. Most politicians are civil *servants*, and they deserve both our prayers and our respect.

That being said, just like clergy and everyone else, sometimes some politicians can be silly. In 2004 a man ran for state office in my home state. Apparently he didn't think his constituents understood English grammar because he campaigned as "a bold conservative." There is honor in being bold, and there is honor in being conservative—but according to *Webster's Dictionary* you can't be both. You have to choose, either bold *or* conservative. Either one is fine, but you've got to choose.

His campaign insulted the voters who apparently recognized it and elected somebody else. His ad was completely *inconsistent*.

That campaign slogan reminded me of the oxymorons we use all the time, as if they made sense.

- A fine mess
- Perfectly awful
- Hot chili
- Inside out
- Pretty ugly

We accept them and use them, though they are completely *inconsistent*.

Not just in our speech but also often in our personal philosophies of life we embrace inconsistencies. Our purpose in this chapter is not to debate a hot topic but simply to use one to illustrate how inconsistent we sometimes are. Many people call themselves "pro-life" but still support capital punishment. How pro-life is that? Many others call themselves "pro-choice" but still oppose capital punishment (the right of collective individuals called the "state" to choose to end a life). How pro-choice is that? If you are serious when you preach about the sanctity of life, does that not by definition include both a fetus and a prisoner on death row? Or, if you are serious when you preach about freedom of choice, must that not apply philosophically to both a particular individual and also to the collective individuals which we call a "state?" This is not to argue for or against either of those positions. It is rather simply to point out the obvious—that most of us are philosophically *inconsistent*.

People are simply like that. How many never know whether their employer is going to be pleasant or hateful? It probably depends on what happened at home at breakfast or the night before. One day he treats you with respect and kindness, and the next day he treats you disrespectfully and inhumanely. Thus, each time you walk into the office, your stomach is tied in knots because you work for someone who is *inconsistent.*

Of course, it is far too easy to point an accusing finger at the rest of the world. The author of Hebrews pointed out that even members of the infant Christian Church were occasionally profoundly inconsistent. Sometimes we still are.

A classmate from seminary serves a beautiful church on the coast of North Carolina. Last summer during vacation I visited him, and he told me about a man he knows in Tennessee. The man is very actively involved in his church and has held virtually every leadership position it has to offer. He is also a mega-wealthy businessman who years ago made a commitment that he would do anything he had to do, ethical or otherwise, to make a lot of money. Not long ago he contacted my friend and said when the time comes, he wants him to officiate at his funeral. As they talked about what he wanted done, the man told Bob: "I want two songs sung, one Christian and one secular. The hymn really describes my faith," the man said, "and the other song really describes my life." They hymn he chose was "Have Thine Own Way, Lord," and the secular song was "I Did It My Way."

"Have Thine Own Way, Lord"/"I Did It My Way." He didn't even recognize the inconsistency.

The author of *Hebrews* talked about Christians who ignore the poor, the imprisoned and the mistreated—Christians who are unfaithful in marriage, who worship money instead of God or who fail to pray for their leaders—Christians who worship God *and* false idols—Christians who preach grace but establish and enforce rigid rules. In short, that New Testament author said that even followers of Christ sometimes say one thing and do another. They are *inconsistent.* And he echoed the question that haunts us: In a world like this where even disciples do not always live consistently, is there anything or anyone we can actually count on? The author continued with what is perhaps the most famous phrase he ever wrote: *"Jesus Christ is the same yesterday, today and for ever."* Meaning that....

– If He said once *"I will be with you always,"* he won't change his mind and abandon us when the tough times come.

– If He said once *"Neither then do I condemn you,"* he won't change his mind when we fail or sin or drop the ball and cast us off as criminals.

– If He said once *"As the Father has loved me, so do I love you,"* he won't change his mind if we lose our job or status or income or self-respect and say, "Now you're not worth loving."

– If He said once *"I have come that you might have life abundant,"* he won't change his mind and decide that he would rather see us suffer instead.

– If He said once *"In my Father's house are many rooms, and I go to prepare a place for you,"* he won't change his mind and let death just be the end of things.

"Jesus Christ is the same yesterday, today and for ever." It means that He can be trusted, that he is divinely *consistent*. He doesn't promise one thing and deliver something else. He is as good as his word. In this world where Emerson said "The only thing constant is change," Jesus is the exception. He does not change the rules on us. He is the one thing we can count on!

Ron Newhouse, that delightful preacher and daily devotional writer, says that a woman in his church was facing very serious surgery and was understandably frightened. Who wouldn't be? The night before she went to the hospital, a friend of hers dropped by for a visit, just to be with her and offer some comfort and encouragement. She asked: "How are you doing?" and Ron's church member confessed: "I am terrified. Every time I think about this surgery, I am scared to death."

Her friend responded: "Do you know how many times the Bible says either *'Fear not'* or *'Be not afraid'*?" The woman answered that she did not. Her friend continued: "Those words - *'Fear not'* or *'Be not afraid'* appear in the Bible 365 times. Not 364 times. And not 366 times. But 365 times, once for every day of the year. It's as if God is saying to us every morning: 'I'm still here. I was here yesterday and the day before that. I'm here today. I'll be here tomorrow and the day after that, too." (from Newhouse's web site, www.devotions.net) Whenever we need him, Jesus promised: *"I will be with you...always!"* He is divinely *consistent*.

A retired United Methodist Bishop, commenting on the formative influences of his life, said: "My father never varied in how he treated my brother, my sister and me. He always expected nothing less than the best from us, and he always forgave us when we failed to live up to those expectations." The strength he received from his father was a sense of consistency—both in moral principles and also in grace.

Jesus is like that. "My father never varied in how he treated my brother, my sister and me," said the retired Bishop. And likewise, Jesus never varies in how he treats us:

Both in his call to moral principle…
And in his willingness to extend grace…
He never varies in His love for us…
His presence with us…
His expectations of us…
His kindness to us…
Or His passion about us.

In a world where "the only thing constant is change," if we are looking for something to count on, that something is Someone. *"Jesus Christ is the same yesterday, today and for ever,"* wrote the author of *Hebrews*. Meaning that He never varies in how he loves us or how he treats us. His presence, grace and compassion are divinely *consistent*.

Study or Discussion Questions

(1) What moral principles best exemplified the life and teachings of Jesus?

(2) What biblical stories call to mind how Jesus was present for those who suffer?

(3) If Jesus were present our community today, what public issues would he champion?

(4) If Jesus were present in our community today, what public or church practices would he challenge?

(5) In a constantly changing world, what is your personal understanding of the text, "*Jesus Christ, the same yesterday, today and forever*?"

GOD WRITES STRAIGHT WITH CROOKED LINES

Read *Philippians 1: 12-26*

In 1981, the late Bishop Ernest Fitzgerald published a book of sermons entitled *God Writes Straight With Crooked Lines*. In that book he told the story of King James I of England, basically a wicked and mentally demented fellow. He was threatened by the popularity of others, so much so that he had people like Sir Walter Raleigh executed. It was said that King James almost never went to bed sober, had few if any friends and possessed the dangerous combination of power *and* madness. Were it not for one decision he made, he would've been remembered only as a despot, if not a derelict. However, an Oxford scholar named John Reynolds suggested to James that there was need for an English translation of the Bible. The king agreed. Seven years later, in 1611, the King James Version of the scriptures was published, and for four hundred years it has had more impact on the world than any other book ever put to print. When Bishop Fitzgerald told that story, he concluded by quoting J.D. Douglas, who said: "How that wicked king was used for a good purpose proves that God has an astonishing capacity for writing straight with crooked lines."

The last half of the opening chapter of *Philippians* makes that point with clarity and power. God has an amazing capacity for taking bad circumstances and creating blessings, or for taking imperfect people and creating ministry. That's what Paul said in the first verses of his letter to the church in Philippi.

(1.) First of all, Paul wrote that **ROSES ARE FOUND AMID THORNS.**

He knew the people in Philippi were about to suffer persecution, and it would be unspeakably difficult for them. But he wrote to tell them that even amid their suffering, there would be silver linings on the clouds if they just looked for them.

Paul wrote his letter from a prison cell under the sentence of death. But consider again what he said: *"I want you to know that what has happened to me has really served to advance the gospel, so that it has become known throughout the entire praetorium guard...."* Because he was imprisoned in Rome, Paul had the chance to preach to Roman guards—government workers—with family members and friends in the city, some in high places. And each time a guard was converted, Paul believed that there was one more chance that a little rock in the waters would create a ripple in the city. Paul honestly believed that his imprisonment would help convert Rome and thus, in time, would help convert the empire.

When former President Jimmy Carter won the Nobel Peace Prize (and it's hard to imagine anyone more deserving) a newspaper columnist commented: "How disappointed Mr. Carter must have been when he lost his bid for re-election. But how blessed the world has been that he was given the chance, unshackled by Capitol Hill, to put his Godly passion into action for people."

Thomas Moore reminds us in his book *Dark Nights Of The Soul that* sometimes in life's toughest moments come our greatest opportunities. Would Ghandi have been remembered but for his self-imposed hunger? Or Helen Keller except for her disabilities? Who do you remember from your childhood, some person whose impact on you has been formative and lasting? Was it an aunt or grandparent who didn't have two nickels to rub together, but they took time to spend with you—and love you—and teach you lessons about living that helped to make you who you are? And if they had been professionally successful and busy, they may not have contributed to your life. Was there some teacher who had dreams of starring on Broadway or singing at The Met, but their dreams never came true? But at your high school, hidden away from the bright lights, they used their talents to inspire in you a love for the arts, an ability to sing or the courage to stand on your feet in front of a crowd?

ABC News carried a story about some exciting breakthroughs in the treatment and training of autistic children. And who came up with these new methodologies that hold so much promise for one child out of five hundred? Two mothers whose sons have autism. We could go on and on, but the point Paul made is clear: Sometimes we find our roses amid life's thorns. As he wrote of his own imprisonment: *"I want you to know that what has happened to me has really served to advance the gospel, so that it has become known throughout the entire praetorium guard…."*

(2.) Second, Paul wrote that **GOD DOES OFTEN WRITE STRAIGHT WITH CROOKED LINES, JUST LIKE HE DID WITH KING JAMES.**

Paul wrote of people who were trying to usurp his authority with the church in Philippi. They thought: "Since Paul is away, we will step in and take over his role and seize the power." So, as he put it: *"Some preach Christ from envy and rivalry…."* But what happened? Paul said: *"In every way, whether in pretense or in truth, Christ is proclaimed; and in that I rejoice!"* In other words, in spite of their imperfections, even in spite of their sins and selfish motives, God did a good thing in Philippi through some people who were not entirely good. I find that inspiring, for it says that if God could use those sinners back then, maybe he can use me, too.

During Clergy Appreciation Month, various families were assigned the privilege (or task) of having the pastor over for lunch on Sundays. One Sunday, as the husband was busy setting the table and the wife was placing bowls of food upon it, little Jeffrey, their five year old, sat and talked with the minister. The pastor asked: "Jeffrey, what has your mom prepared for lunch?" The five year old answered: "We're having goat." That being somewhat surprising, the preacher said: "Son, are you sure about that?," to which little Jeffrey replied: "Yep. I heard her tell

Daddy not to play golf today because we're having the old goat for lunch!"

To be honest, most of us preachers have been called worse. So, I suspect, have some laity. But look at the list of people God used to build The Kingdom: *Abraham,* a drunken adulterer...*Jacob,* a liar and thief...*Moses,* a murderer...*David,* an adulterous murderer...*Simon Peter,* who denied even knowing Jesus when the chips were down...*Paul,* a persecutor of Christians and an accomplice to murder. And, not to be sexist, there are others like *Ruth, Mary Magdalene* and *the woman at the well.* The list goes on of how God used genuinely imperfect people to accomplish a holy purpose, which means that you and I do not have to be perfect in order to be useful.

"Just as I am Thou wilt receive
Wilt welcome, pardon, cleanse, relieve."

And, not only will God "welcome, pardon, cleanse, relieve," but he will also use us to love and help people, to heal hurts and champion causes, to strengthen the church and also the community. If we open ourselves to God, he has a purpose for us, even those of us who are profoundly imperfect. "God Writes Straight With Crooked Lines."

(3.) Finally, Paul wrote that **EVEN DEATH DOES NOT DEFEAT THOSE WHO BELIEVE.**

Paul wrote to the Philippians from prison sentenced to die. He did not want to die and hoped his sentence would be overturned. But he knew full well what could (and probably would) happen. And in face of that, he wrote: *"...now as always Christ will be exalted in my body, whether by life or by death. For me, to live is Christ and to die is gain."*

Talk about writing with a "crooked line!" Paul was facing death, the ultimate defeat, the end of all his hopes and dreams. But here he says, "No! It is not the end! By the power of Christ, *'to die is gain'.*"

Ministers baptize beautiful babies in morning services and officiate at funeral services for the aged in the afternoon. In a single day in church we act out the script: *"The Lord giveth, and the Lord taketh away."* But what if that is not true? What if what we witness in baptisms *and* memorial services are simply proofs of the words, *"The Lord giveth...?"* Maybe all we have observed are actually evidences of new birth, new life and new futures. Isn't that what our faith says? Martin Luther King, Jr. is famous, among other things, for having said: "I shall die only once, but I shall be born twice." Life, death, and then life again unfettered by sickness, sadness or goodbyes.

In Valladolid, Spain, where Christopher Columbus died in 1506, there is a monument commemorating the great discoverer. Perhaps the most interesting feature of the memorial is a statue of a lion destroying one of the words that had been part of Spain's motto for centuries. Before Columbus made his voyages, the Spaniards thought that they lived on the outer edge of earth. Thus for years their national motto was "No More Beyond." The lion on the memorial statue is tearing away the word "No." It was their way of saying that Columbus had proven that there was "More Beyond."

Jesus proved it long before Columbus—that when life ends here, it is simply a time of new birth in a new Place where life shall never end. "I shall die only once, but I shall be born twice." That is basically what Paul told the Philippians who were already grieving for him as he faced execution. *"Now as always Christ will be exalted in my body, whether by life or by death,"* he said. *"For me, to live is Christ and to die is gain."* It was Paul's way of saying that there is "more beyond."

St. Paul and Ernest Fitzgerald were on the same page. Both believed that "God Writes Straight With Crooked Lines." That's what this lesson from *Philippians* says:

– That sometimes in life bad circumstances produce blessings;

– That sinful people can be used for saintly purposes; and,

– That even death is merely a doorway to life that never ends.

Study or Discussion Questions

(1) How does one overcome personal inadequacies in order to "succeed" in life (personally, professionally, relationally, and spiritually)?

(2) Is it possible to use one's weaknesses, or hardships in ways that produce positive results? (In other words, how can one turn lemons into lemonade?)

(3) Discuss or consider how the Apostle Paul compensated for personal weaknesses in his life of ministry.

(4) How can adult role models (parents, grandparents, teachers, coaches, tutors, etc) encourage children and youth to cope with and perhaps even overcome personal limitations?

(5) What difficulties faced Jesus as he performed his ministry? How did He deal with them?

MANAGING THE MINNOWS

Read *Matthew 23: 24-28*

There is an old adage that says: "Very few of us are ever swallowed by whales. Instead, most of us are nibbled to death by minnows." Or, as another proverb puts it: "The devil is in the details."

Who would argue that life is too often dominated by details, by little things that nibble away at our time and energy like minnows? So, how do we keep it from happening? How do we protect ourselves from being so overwhelmed by a thousand little things that we never get around to the handful of other things that really matter?

United Methodist Bishop Bevel Jones frequently says: "The main thing is to keep the main thing the main thing!"

A time-management consultant on *The Today Show* talked about interruptions in the work place. She said one a key to success in business is to enter the office every morning and ask: "What is the primary task before me today? What is the most important thing I have been hired to do?" Then, she said, address that task and tend to interruptions only after the primary task has been done. "Otherwise," she said, "an endless barrage of little things will get in the way of the main thing."

So, how do we do it? How do we keep our lives from being nibbled to death by minnows?

Here is what it looks like for clergy. My first Callings from God are to preach, to teach and to envision ministry. In truth, a church is not a corporation, and a pastor is not a CEO. I am a preacher. Preparing to preach with any sort of intelligibility is an exacting and time-consuming task. George Buttrick, the great minister of Madison Avenue Presbyterian Church in New York City, and later Professor of Preaching at Southern Seminary in Louisville, instructed his students that every minute in the pulpit should represent an hour in the study. That may be somewhat exaggerated, but the point remains that one cannot ignore the importance of being prepared.

A minister decided that he was wasting a lot of time preparing sermons. "After all," he thought, "God is the real preacher. I'm just the vehicle. It is almost unfaithful for me to work on sermons and not give God the chance to say what he wants to say. So, I'm not going to do it anymore." All week long, the preacher had a great time. No time spent studying, writing, editing, re-writing or memorizing. Instead, he played golf five times that week. On Sunday morning he stood to preach. Before stepping behind the pulpit, he bowed his head and said: "O Lord, what do you want me to tell these people today?" In the silence he heard the Lord's voice answer: "Why don't you tell them how to putt!"

Sermons do not "just happen." They require time and lots of it. I personally prepare two different messages every week, and it is exacting work. And yet, every preacher alive will confess that sometimes our first Calling is the last thing we get around to because time for study and preparation gets crowded out by other things, like countless meetings or offices with revolving doors. A well respected United Methodist minister hangs a sign on his office door every weekday morning from 8:00 – noon. It says: "If somebody died, please come in." It is his way of saying that he is committed to putting first things first, that he owes it to God and to his people to be prepared for preaching. He resists interruptions in order to keep the main thing the main thing.

Enough about preachers. What about you? What does it mean to you to honor your Calling to put first things first? What does it mean to you to prioritize in life so that your time, your energy and your soul don't get nibbled to death by minnows?

I read of a mother and father who became Co-Chairs of a Community Bridge Association. They served a two year stint. The association sponsored bridge tournaments and bridge clubs all over town. The couple, as Co-Chairs, was at some related event on the average of four nights a week. During their time in office, their teenaged daughter began to distribute illegal drugs out of their home because mama and daddy were never there to notice. But they did notice one night when they arrived home and saw blue lights, and watched as their daughter was led in handcuffs to a squad car. She went to jail because her parents let lesser things take precedence over the main thing.

Years ago a young man came to my office in tears. He had gone home unexpectedly one afternoon and found his wife in a romantic situation with a neighbor, much like a scene from *Desperate Housewives*. He came to see me emotionally devastated. But, surprisingly, his anger seemed more directed at himself than at his wife. He told me that for five years he had played golf every afternoon Monday through Friday, and usually stayed late at the club grill afterward for a burger with his friends. He wept and confessed: "I treated my wife like a single mother for so long that she obviously began to feel single." He had let lesser issues take precedence over the main thing.

It is not that the other things in life are evil or unimportant. But when we fail to prioritize, when we fail to put first things first, we are gambling with the soul of life. We are allowing ourselves to be nibbled to death by minnows.

Jesus knew it happens, sometimes even among good and well-meaning people. The gospel of *Matthew* says He challenged Pharisees. Not the thieves and ax murderers, but Pharisees. Church leaders. The most religious people you could hope to meet back then. People who not only strictly observed The Ten Commandments, but observed over six hundred other commandments in addition.

A colleague in the ministry told me of a conversation he had with a notorious man in his church. The man was a Christmas-and-Easter member who the rest of the time led an unbelievably "colorful" life. The minister said to him: "How can you be so unconcerned about keeping The Ten Commandments?" The man answered:

"Preacher, I'm not unconcerned. At one time or another in my life, I've kept all of them!"

The Pharisees would have fainted dead away at that. No one was more concerned with living righteously than they were. But those were the very people Jesus challenged at the point of their priorities. *"You blind guides,"* He said. *"You strain at a gnat and swallow a camel! Woe to you, scribes and Pharisees, hypocrites! You (worry about rules and regulations on how to) cleanse the outside of the cup and plate, but inside (you hardly even notice things like) extortion and greed."* They did not answer the Calling to keep the main thing the main thing. They allowed lesser issues to crowd out the issues that ultimately mattered most.

Like those Pharisees, most "religious people" are not immune to doing that. We say Jesus is first for us (as he should be) but our actions sometimes fail to back up our words. We too often let good things get in the way of the main thing.

How many folks do not have enough time to take a job in the church, but they have plenty of time to work for their civic club?

How many of us do not have enough time to allot a few minutes each day to prayer or reading the Bible, but we have plenty of time for watching *Monday Night Football* or *American Idol*?

How many folks give more money each year to their alma mater or the country club or their wardrobes or their vacation plans than they give to the church, and it never even occurs to them that when they write their checks, God himself observes their priorities?

Someone told me of being so moved by the plight of the victims of Hurricane Katrina that she sent $100 to the Red Cross. In the same conversation she told me of hiring a new ballet teacher for "only $4000 a year." Priorities.

"Woe to you, scribes and Pharisees, hypocrites! You strain at a gnat and swallow a camel!" Do not misinterpret. Your civic club, and your TV shows, and your country clubs, and your alma maters are probably worthy of your investments. But sometimes even "religious people" ignore their primary Callings and allow good things to take precedence over God's things.

That advice, of course, is not just appropriate for individual Christians but for congregations, as well. Sometimes the temptation confronts churches to major in minors, to become absorbed to the point of being obsessed with issues that are not "the main thing."

Peter Drucker taught with such clarity and power that the core purpose of a non-profit is to change lives. In how many church committee meetings does that topic even come up? We talk about important things like budgets, governance models and facility issues. But how often in church meetings or in Sunday School classes do we talk about what we are doing to change lives? *"Woe to you, scribes and Pharisees, hypocrites! You strain at a gnat and swallow a camel!"* You do not keep the main thing the main thing.

Walking out of a restaurant with some church members, we noticed a sign near the door. It said: "Success does not happen by accident." Jesus said that to the Pharisees. Bevel Jones says it to his audiences. Life says it eloquently and powerfully when it comes to our professions, our relationships and our faith: Success, happiness, fulfillment do not come by accident. They come only when we say Yes to our primary Calling—to keep the main thing the main thing.

Study or Discussion Questions

(1) In your personal life, indentify pressing matters that distract you from crucial matters.

(2) Identify issues in the life of congregations that distract churches from authentic ministry.

(3) Discuss the roles of prayer, scripture and conversation with persons of Faith in adequately prioritizing in one's life or the life of a church.

(4) What must an individual or church sacrifice in order to honor those priorities?

(5) At the end of your life's journey, what do you want to look back and be able to say? How can you make that happen?

FACET FOUR: *PERSONAL DISCIPLESHIP*

LIVING AS A DISCIPLE

Read *Luke 10: 1-17*

Some time ago someone sent me a list of answers that showed up on college exams in a religion course. The article claimed that these are honest-to-goodness answers that college students gave on tests:

When asked, "What are the four gospels?," one student answered: "John, Paul, George and Ringo."

Another student got two Bible stories confused and described Lot's wife as "A pillar of salt by day and a ball of fire by night."

When asked, "Who were the epistles?," one student answered: "They were the wives of the apostles."

And, when asked to name the disciples, one student answered: "Peter, James, John, Paul, Martin Luther, Billy Graham, Mother Theresa and also I think my grandmother was a pretty good disciple."

The student gave the wrong answer so far as the professor was concerned. Paul, an apostle, was not one of the twelve disciples. Neither were Luther, Graham, Mother Theresa or the boy's grandma. But, at a deeper level—and, in fact, at a biblical level—he was absolutely on target.

Luke refers to seventy unnamed, anonymous servants of Christ whom he called "disciples." The story appears in the tenth chapter of his gospel. Were one to read the ninth chapter, they would run across stories about how pressured and pushed the original twelve disciples were—feeding the five thousand, struggling to figure out the nature and mission of Jesus, trying desperately and unsuccessfully to escape from the pressing crowds and just rest and breathe a little, going from village to village and houses to house, healing the sick and preaching the Good News and sometimes being persecuted and rejected, trying to heal an epileptic child. A person can get tired just reading the ninth chapter of *Luke* and all that Jesus and those twelve men were trying to do. So, chapter ten begins by saying: *"After this, the Lord appointed seventy others, and sent them on ahead of him, two by two, into every town and place where he himself was to come. And he said to them, 'The harvest is plentiful, but the laborers are few....'"*

My mother's first cousin was a man named Jake Early. Though he was actually my second cousin, everyone in the family called him "Uncle Jake." For ten years, Uncle Jake was the catcher for the Washington Senators in the Major Leagues. One year, he even started for the American League All Star team. Anyway, Jake said one of his favorite people in the world was a man named Tony Giuliana. Tony Giuliana was Jake's back-up catcher. He was the guy who would play the second half of a double-header. He was the one who late in the season would spell Uncle Jake for a game or two, allowing his knees to rest and heal a little. Jake said: "No catcher can carry a team on his own shoulders for a full season. Everyone needs someone like Tony, ready to put on the pads....everyone needs someone like Tony, ready to put on the pads."

Even the twelve disciples apparently needed their own version of Tony, other believers who would put on the pads, other disciples who would share the responsibility of healing the sick and preaching The Word.

The biography of George Washington, *His Excellency*, tells how Washington, when trying to form a republic and organize a government, was opposed by former friends like Thomas Jefferson and James Madison who sought to undermine his efforts. But, Alexander Hamilton stood by Washington. He was an ally Washington could trust. He went out pleading his cause and preaching his vision. Washington said he kept the course because Hamilton was in his corner. Even the original twelve disciples needed their own versions of Alexander Hamilton, people who were in their corner, their own versions of Tony Guiliana, people who would put on the pads and help them in the overwhelming work of building God's Kingdom.

"After this, the Lord appointed seventy others, and sent them on ahead of him, two by two, into every town and place where he himself was to come. And he said to them, 'The harvest is plentiful, but the laborers are few....'" So there they went, that anonymous band of disciples (fishers and

carpenters and tent-makers and uncles and aunts and grandmothers) serving Christ and loving people. And later the story says: *"The seventy returned with joy, saying, 'Lord, even the demons are subject to us in your name!'"* The beautiful point of that story is simply to say that the young man on the Religion test was right: Billy Graham and Mother Theresa and his grandma and all the faithful believers throughout the years who tried their best to serve Christ and love people are all "disciples!"

You do not have to be famous to be a disciple. You do not have to be theologically trained (so far as I know, none of the original disciples were). You do not have to hold a position of power in the community or in the church. All you have to be is faithful. Faithful…and maybe alert. If we keep the eyes of our souls open, we will find opportunities for ministry surrounding us at every corner.

I read a father's story about his daughter when she was a pre-schooler. One night, after watching a scary show on TV, the little girl who was afraid to go to bed. She told her parents she didn't like being all alone up there. After three or four trips to her parents' room, her dad tried to reassure her by saying: "Look, honey, you are not really alone in your bedroom. God is watching over you. He is everywhere. In fact, He's in your bedroom with you," he said his little girl almost timidly walked back upstairs, stood outside her bedroom door, and her parents heard her say: "God, if you are in there, please don't say anything. It would scare me to death!"

Expanding that father's advice just a little: Not only is God everywhere, but opportunities to serve God are also everywhere. At every hand. In almost every situation.

All the time. As our *Luke* put it, *"The harvest is plentiful."* You don't have to look very far before you find an opportunity to practice your discipleship!

A former church member of mine was a supervisor in a textile mill. He said whereas most of the other supervisors went out or went home for lunch every day, instead about four days a week he carries a sandwich and sits in the break room where the floor workers eat. He said he will pick out one or two different people every day, call their name, and simply ask the question: "How's life treating you?" He reported: "You wouldn't believe how many times people open up when they hear that one question. They talk to me about the stresses they're carrying—about their lives at home, their financial problems, their aging parents, their reckless children, their depression, their fears. And almost every time before the lunch break is over, they will say, 'Thanks for listening. I feel better just having talked about it.' Those lunch breaks," he said, "are my ministry." In the break room of a textile mill he practices discipleship.

A friend of mine is the president of a lovely United Methodist College in Greensboro, North Carolina. He is one of the finest educators and one of the finest men I know. Over lunch one day he talked to me about his relationships with the students at his college. He said by the end of the year, he manages to know the name of virtually every student on campus. I asked him how a college president could pull that off, and he said he goes to all the football games and basketball games, but instead of sitting in a President's Box, he sits in the stands with the students and gets to know them. He also said that every day he eats breakfast and most days lunch with the students in the campus cafeteria. I asked only half-jokingly: "You actually choose to eat cafeteria food?," to which he answered: "I choose to be with those kids. Most of them are away from home, and sometimes they're worried and no longer have mom or dad to turn to. So, I try to be around if they need to turn to me." In the cafeteria of a United Methodist college, he practices discipleship.

"The harvest is plentiful." And you do not have to be Peter, James or John or even Billy Graham or Mother Theresa to do something about it. All of us who sometimes feel like nothing more than back-up catchers and who never grab the headlines can still make a difference for Christ in the world. As long as we are around people, we are surrounded by needs. Some are dramatic, as with the hungry and homeless. Others are far better disguised. But sometimes nothing more than a simple question, "How's the world treating you?," will tear those disguises away...and reveal a human heart broken with pain...and will provide us with an urgent place to practice our discipleship.

Study or Discussion Questions

(1) Name five persons from the Bible or church history whom you consider to have been authentic disciples. What did each of them do to warrant your opinion?

A
B
C
D
E

(2) Name three persons from your childhood or youth who had formative positive influences on you. What did each of them do to warrant your opinion?
A
B
C

(3) What is the best skill or gift you possess that can be used in your life of discipleship?

(4) In what ways are you currently using that gift?

(5) Who has been a "helper in the shadows" for you (a person who has strengthened your life but has received little or no credit for doing so)? How can you make that person feel valued?

STEPPING OUT OF THE BOAT

Read *Matthew 14: 22-33*

To be properly understood, every biblical text must be read in context. The story of the disciples adrift in a stormy sea comes immediately after the feeding of the five thousand.

Since Jesus seated the five thousand *"on the green grass,"* we can be certain in that area it was springtime.

Since the miracle of the meal occurred in Galilee, we can be sure the story of Christ s walking on the water took place on the Sea of Galilee (which, of course, is not actually a sea, but rather a large lake).

In the spring, violent storms descend without warning on the Sea of Galilee. Experienced fishermen would not go out during a violent storm, nor even if one were predicted. But during spring on that lake, the storms come suddenly and with no warning.

Since the story says this occurred *"in the fourth watch of the night,"* we know it must have happened about 3:00 a.m. Probably there was a full moon, which would explain how Jesus knew his friends were in trouble. He had sent them on ahead of him while he went into the hills to pray. But He could see them, sailing in the moonlight. And thus He could see when the storm arose and his friends were in peril.

And so He came to them. In the Greek, the word for *"walking on the water"* also can be translated *"walking to the water."* Depending on how you feel about literal miracles, take your choice. Either translation is accurate. The point is that when they were in trouble, Jesus came to them, as he does to us.

When the disciples saw Jesus walking in their direction at 3:00 a.m. in the moonlight in a storm, they said: *"It is a ghost!"* One might think that was not very enlightened of them, maybe not even particularly Christian. But, those were superstitious times. In that day and age, crises were associated with spirits or demons. Probably they assumed that the demon who had stirred the storm was coming after them. Given the same set of circumstances, we might also have thought we were seeing a ghost or a spirit.

One of the disciples present in the boat was Simon Peter. He was always impulsive and sometimes unwise, but he at least had sufficient faith to step out of the boat. *"'Lord, if it is you,' he said, 'tell me to come to you on the water.' 'Come,' said Jesus. Then Peter got down out of the boat, walked on the water and came toward Christ."*

In theological terms, "faith" and "trust" are virtually synonymous. It is one thing to say, "I believe there is a

God out there somewhere." That is, after all, a statement of intellectual faith. But a person of heart-felt faith is able to say, "Not only do I believe that there is a God out there somewhere, but I also believe that God loves me and cares for me, and I am safe in his hands." That is a statement of trust. Obviously that is what Simon Peter had when he ran the risk of stepping out of the boat.

Many of us remember standing in a swimming pool and saying, "One, two, three jump!," whereupon our little child would hurl himself into our arms in the water. Had you failed to catch him, your child may have drowned. But your son or daughter knew down deep in the heart (they trusted) that Mommy or Daddy would never let them down. That's what "faith" is: *trust* that a Heavenly Parent loves us and will catch us when we fall.

Across the years I have heard so many persons facing serious medical treatments or surgery say: "I'm really not too frightened. I have all the confidence in the world in my doctor." That is what "faith" is: the ability in all circumstances to *trust* our lives and well-being to the hands of "the Great Physician."

So, what does this biblical story say to persons of faith in our lives here and now? It says simply that life can be safe and uneventful if we never venture from where we are. But excitement, adventure and accomplishment are reserved for those who, trusting in Christ, step out of the boat.

A popular actor/comedian confessed on a talk show that, as a child, he did not have the strongest of relationships with his father. When he decided to go into show business, his dad was discouraging. "Why would you do a thing like that?," he asked. "What makes you think you have the talent? You'll starve. Be smart. Be safe. Stay home and work in the store." But fortunately for those who have loved his movies across decades, Jerry Lewis decided not to play it safe but rather to step out of the boat.

Brett Butler was not offered a baseball scholarship to the college where he wanted to go. The coach said, "You may have been good in high school, but you're too small to play at this level. Go get a degree in business or something." How foolish that coach must have felt when Brett Butler went on to play seventeen years in the Major Leagues, even starting for the National League All Stars when he was with the Dodgers. Butler defied logic and decided instead to step out of the boat.

Thomas Edison was told he was uneducable. Colonel Sanders was a failure in business, past the age of retirement, and bankrupt when he decided to give it one more shot by frying chicken. Often the difference between success and failure is simply the resolve some people have to step out of the boat, to pursue a dream, or to follow through on a commitment.

An I.R.S. agent who one day came to visit a pastor. The agent explained that he was auditing the tax returns of a member of the pastor's church. "Reverend," the agent said, "I ran across something a little curious in the returns. This man claims to have donated $100,000 to your church this year. I just wanted to know if he has really given that much." The minister answered quickly: "I can assure you, if he hasn't given it yet, he will!" Too many of us make commitments but don't follow through. We dream noble dreams without the courage to pursue them.

I have a friend who is now retired but had an indescribably successful career in ministry. He went into church after church and led periods of growth and renewal that were little short of miraculous. The last church to which he was assigned before retirement was a place on the edge of a desert. It was a town about 100,000 residents. The church was a nice, comfortable congregation of about a thousand members. Pleasant. Calm. Manageable. The bishop assumed it would not be too taxing on a man about to call it quits. When my friend retired, that church had gone through four facility expansions and was averaging over four thousand people at worship every week. I asked him how he could pull that off church after church, and he answered: "Some people are satisfied just to manage the store. God has always pushed me to build the business."

It is too easy and ever so safe just "to manage the store," just to keep things going the way they've always gone. But, as Herb Miller rightly and consistently advises: "If you always do what you've always done, you'll always get what you've always had." We are called to more than that. As I am often reminded by a clergy friend: "Faith that takes no risks is not faithful."

Where, then, is Christ calling you to do something new and bold in your life? Where might He be calling you to step out of the boat? It is undeniably scary when we take that step. Even Simon Peter became frightened and felt that he was about to sink, but Jesus was there, extending a hand, holding on and keeping him safe. Trusting that Christ is with us in that same way, where do you feel he is calling you to do something new and bold in or through your own life? Where might He be calling you to step out of the boat?

Could it be in your business or career that you might be called to take a new risk? To grow? To expand? Perhaps even to change from one career to another? Have you felt a tugging at your soul to do more than just maintain?

In your family life or your primary relationships? Who are you taking for granted? With whom are you afraid to be honest? How often and why are you failing to show your love while there is still time? And how will you feel if you wait too long to step out of the boat?

In your personal spirituality? Do you feel challenged to explore the Bible with an open mind? Is there some reason you re afraid to pray by listening to God instead of talking at him?

In the use of your leisure time? Is it possible Jesus is calling you to step out of the comfort of your boat and into the deep waters where people suffer, perhaps by volunteering to tutor a child or visit a shut-in, to work with Hospice or Habitat for Humanity? You fill in the blanks.

At church? How in that community does Christ call people to step out of the boat? To reach out to and love those who are different? To become seriously evangelistic? To decide that there is more to ministry than maintaining the store, but rather we are called to build God s business in new ways with passion and compassion? Do you feel a personal calling to play a bigger role, to stretch yourself, to do something that makes your church better and stronger than it s ever been before?

In every key area of life, Herb Miller was right. If we settle for always doing what we have always done, we will always get what we have always had. There ought to be more to life than that. Life and faith become real when we trust Christ enough to take his hand and boldly step out of the boat. I do not know how that opportunity will come to you this day, nor about what topic in your life, but this much I do know: at some point virtually every day that opportunity comes.

Study or Discussion Questions

Discuss or meditate upon the following five quotes:

(1) "Courage is the price that Life exacts for granting peace." – Amelia Earhardt

(2) "Courage and perseverance have a magical talisman, before which difficulties disappear and obstacles vanish into air." – John Quincy Adams

(3) "Courage is doing what you're afraid to do; there can be no courage unless your're scared." – Eddie Rickenbacker

(4) "I've come to believe that each of us has a personal calling that's as unique as a fingerprint – and the best way to succeed is to discover what you love and then find a way to offer it to others in the form of service, working

hard, and also allowing the energy of the Universe to lead you". – Oprah Winfrey

(5) "Those who would save their lives shall lose them, but whoever would lose his life for my sake, the same shall find it."– Jesus

EVEN WE CAN BE INSTRUMENTS OF GRACE

Read *Philippians 3: 1-14*

Recently I browsed through a catalogue from a Christian Speakers' Bureau in Nashville. They represent people like Margaret Bush, Bobby Bowden, Joe Torre, Jack Canfield and a host of well known people who go around the country making their witness. One name listed was a man named Michael (last name will be withheld here). His bio read that his father was mafia figure in New York City. Michael grew up in that environment. When he finished college, he went off to med school. But during that time, his dad died. So Michael came back to New York and assumed his dad's post as a leader in organized crime. Eventually he was arrested, convicted of various crimes and sent to prison for seven years. There he was—a young man, his whole history being involved with organized crime, his future devoted to it, sitting behind bars at Attica. One night an inmate said to him, "You got big problems, brother. Why don't you turn them over to God?"

Michael initially laughed at the idea and answered, "What have I ever done that would get God on my side?"

The older man replied, "That's the beauty of it. He's on your side before you do the first thing."

That inmate at Attica accurately described the wonder of "grace." God is on your side before you do the first thing. It was a turning point for Michael who did not go back to organized crime but rather goes out all across America telling people about the unearned, transforming love of Jesus Christ who is on our side before we do the first thing.

Paul had done churchy things before becoming a Christian. As he told the *Philippians*, he had been ceremoniously marked as a Jew *"on the eighth day, (I was) of the people of Israel, of the tribe of Benjamin, a Hebrew of Hebrews, a law-abiding Pharisee…."* But, despite outward appearances, Paul admitted that down deep in his heart were other things: things like anger, jealousy, arrogance, prejudice and hatred. As he wrote, he was *"a persecutor of Christians"* and had been an accomplice to the murder of St. Stephen. In fact, there was so much darkness and despair in his soul that in Paul's words, he said he felt like *"the chief of sinners."* But then something happened. Jesus reached down on the road to Damascus, hugged Paul to himself, held him close, whispered to him of forgiveness, and turned all the darkness inside him to light. Paul told the Philippians that everything he had been before he considered *"as rubbish,"* but he rejoiced, as he put it, that

I do *"not have a righteousness of my own…but that which is through faith in Christ!"*

What did that mean? It meant that Paul finally figured out, as the bumper sticker puts it, that "God Loves Us Anyhow!" We don't have to be good enough, moral enough, smart enough, rich enough or anything enough. God's love comes to us not "because of" what we are, but "in spite of" it. Paul learned that Jesus was on his side before he did the first thing.

A second grade Sunday School teacher in Arizona named Mildred wrote in a devotional magazine some time ago of having her students do a month long prayer journal—writing down each prayer they prayed throughout the whole month. Once they were turned in, she read through them. In the journal of one of the little boys in her class was this entry: "Dear God, please ignore my mom's prayers to make me a better boy. I'm sure You and I are pretty happy with me the way I am!" That child must have read *Philippians*. He understood that God loves us in spite of ourselves. He is on our side before we do the first thing.

"Just as I am Thou wilt receive!"

There is another thing Paul wanted the *Philippians* to understand. Paul wrote from a prison cell to people who were by-and-large impoverished and facing a coming Roman persecution. He wrote as one who suffers to people who suffer. As such he reminded them that grace is the presence of Christ with us in life's tough times. He said that we *"share in the sufferings of Christ…so somehow to attain the resurrection of the dead."* Jesus suffered like we do, said Paul, so he understands what we experience when we hurt. And His sufferings wound up in victory (the Resurrection) meaning that our sufferings can wind up in victory, too. Paul reminded the *Philippians* that grace is the presence of Christ with us in life's tough times.

How hard it must have been on Laci Peterson's family as her due date approached and she had not then been recovered. Each passing day made it less and less likely she ever would be. How proud her family was of that young wife and mom-to-be. And how devastated they were in the wake of her disappearance and ultimate death.

Our nation mourned, but especially the family members of seven astronauts on board the Columbia mourned their tragic death. How proud they were of their loved ones making that mission. And how broken hearted they must have been in the wake of the crash.

How loving and concerned are spouses and parents of soldiers involved in the military action in Iraq. How crushed some of those loved ones are when the ongoing flood of death notices are received.

Or what of the parents in Alabama whose children were killed when a tornado collapsed the roof to their high school?

Is there a word for those who hurt and grieve? There is no quick fix. But there is a word, and it is this: Jesus is with us in our suffering, and even in the face of death, there is still victory. Isn't that what Paul told the *Philippians*? We *"share in the sufferings of Christ...so somehow to attain the resurrection of the dead."* In our pain, He is with us, and someday beyond the final pain we will be with him! As the President said of the fallen astronauts, "The crew of the space shuttle Columbia did not return safely to the earth. But we can pray that they are safely at Home."

Having said a word about Grace, Paul went on to say a word about Discipleship. *"Forgetting what is behind, and straining forward to what is ahead, I press on toward the goal for the upward prize in Christ Jesus."*

One of the best people I know was for a while profane, violent, dishonest, and frequently in trouble with the police. Today he is a leader in his community and his church, the sort of person I would trust my life to without thinking twice. Some time ago he talked about his dramatic turn-around. He credits it all to his wife. He said: "She loved me so much when I was bad that I started trying to be good, just for her."

So felt Paul about his life of discipleship. Christ loved him so much when he was bad that for the rest of his life he tried to be good, just for Jesus. *"Forgetting what is behind, and straining forward to what is ahead, I press on toward the goal for the upward prize in Christ Jesus."* We do not live Christian lives to earn God's love; instead, we are so overwhelmed by and thankful for that love that we live Christian lives just for him. Grace comes first. Discipleship is our response to it. It is like the story of the Prodigal. The father loved him even when he was in the far country, and eventually it was the knowledge of that father's love which brought the boy back home.

Recently I was sent an internet story attributed to Max Lucado. It was about Maria and Christina, a mother and daughter from Brazil. Christina was a strong-willed child, and Maria was a devoted mother. When Christina was sixteen, she and her mom got into an argument whereupon the young girl walked out of their poor home, claiming she would live her own life and make her own rules. Maria knew that a teenaged girl with little education would quickly sink to the bottom of life, just to survive. She would fall into the drug culture or into prostitution. So, Maria set out in search of her daughter.

Before she began her journey, Maria took what little money she had to a local store where there was a photograph booth—the kind you sometimes find in K-Mart or Wal-Mart. She used all her money to make a stack of black and white pictures of herself. Then Maria began going from city to city in Brazil, hitting all the bars and hotels and taping her picture in lobbies and women's rooms.

Her suspicions about her daughter were accurate. Christina had fallen into prostitution just to stay alive. One evening she walked down a long flight of steps in a Brazilian hotel, and at the bottom she saw a familiar face. Taped to a mirror next to the bar was a picture of her mother. Christina walked over to the mirror and pulled the picture off. When she turned it over, there was a hand-scribbled message from Maria. It simply said: "I don't care what you've done. Please come home." Christina took the money in her purse, bought a bus ticket and went home.

That is grace. God doesn't care what we've done or failed to do. He keeps the door open and the lights on, hoping his prodigal children will come home.

That's what Paul told the *Philippians* in chapter three of this wonderful book. Grace (God's unconditional love for us, his open heart and open arms) comes first. And once we finally realize how deeply we are loved, we begin the journey home. *"Forgetting what is behind, and straining forward to what is ahead, I press on toward the goal for the upward prize in Christ Jesus."*

Study or Discussion Questions

(1) Define your biblical/theological understanding of the word "Grace."

(2) Define your biblical/theological understanding of the word "Transformation." Identify a biblical character whose life was positively transformed. Defend your answer.

(3) What can a person learn from the memory of his/her sins?

(4) Discuss or mediate upon the three main characters in Jesus' parable of *The Prodigal Son*. Identify strengths of each character.

(5) "Sanctification" is a Wesleyan principle indicating "the process of being made perfect."

(A) How can you sense that principle being live out in your own life?

(B) How do disciples cope with/live within the limitations of their humanity?

SIMPLY LOVING

Read *Mark 12: 28-34*

A five-year-old walked into the den where his dad was reading the paper. In a very straightforward way, the child asked: "Daddy, where did I come from?" The father gulped, thinking that this inevitable question had come a lot sooner than he expected it would, but proceeded to go ahead and answer as accurately as he knew how. So, delicately but honestly he walked his five-year-old son through the story of the birds and the bees. The little boy just stood there saying nothing. Then he turned and walked into the kitchen. His dad heard him say to his mom, "Mommy, where did I come from?" The mom answered, "Baltimore," to which her son said, "Thanks, Mommy. I asked Daddy, but he didn't have a clue!"

Sometimes, albeit from well-meaning motives, we complicate things far more than needs to be.

Karl Barth was one of the five premier theologians of the twentieth century. Along with Paul Tillich, Rudolph Bultmann, Dietrich Bonehoeffer and Reinhold Niebuhr, Barth helped articulate neo-orthodoxy in a way it had not been communicated since the days of Luther. Barth's *Dogmatics* is still required reading in most seminaries since it spells out the particulars of Christian doctrine more powerfully than any book since the Bible itself. Barth was, in short, a theological genius.

In the early part of the twentieth century, Dr. Barth was asked to lecture at the University of Chicago Theological School, one of the finest and most scholarly seminaries in the nation. His message that night was appropriately brilliant and deep. Afterward, there was a time for questions-and-answers. A young Ph.D. student asked: "Dr Barth, can you state for us the central thesis of Christian faith?" Everyone expected something so cerebral that they would have to run for their dictionaries to figure it out. Instead, Karl Barth took a deep breath and answered, "As I see it, the central thesis of the Christian faith is this: 'Jesus loves me, this I know, for the Bible tells me so.'" When all the scholarship had been explored and exhausted, that great theologian got down to the simplicity of it all. For Barth, the bottom line of faith was simply love.

At the end of the day, most of us are looking for a simple, understandable word about life and faith. While theological exploration and study are indispensable for Christian growth, at some point we still long to hear it put simply.

That explains a great deal of the popularity of Billy Graham. He has always understood our need to hear faith clearly stated. To a great extent, that is why he attracted such massive crowds. His message is simple, clear, and easy to understand. Every time you hear him preach, the message is: *"You must be born again."* Dr. Graham says himself that basically he has just that one sermon and simply changes the illustrations.

Simplicity," it is said, "is the queen of the virtues." Surely not only Barth and Graham but also Jesus himself would have agreed. No one has ever possessed nor will they ever possess the wisdom of Christ. The New Testament says: *"In the beginning was the Logos* (i.e., 'the mind of God')*...and the logos became flesh and dwelt among us."* In other words, Jesus had within himself the very wisdom of God. More than anyone else who ever lived or shall, He was infinitely capable of soaring above the heads of his listeners, had he chosen to do so. But when a scribe asked him what faith and discipleship were all about, Jesus answered simply: *"You shall love the Lord your God...and you shall love your neighbor as yourself."* At the end of the day, said Jesus, all thought, talk and practice of faith boil down to love.

It really is that simple. "Jesus loves me, this I know."

"You shall love the Lord your God...and you shall love your neighbor as yourself." However deep and scholarly our faith is (and it is), ultimately it all boils down to love.

Far too many buy into the myth that life is about money. Truly wise people know better. We really cannot take it with us. An old man was dying. He went to the bank and had his multiple millions translated into a cashier's check made out to himself. He left just enough in his account for his widow to scrape by after he died. He took the cashier's check, put it in an envelope and placed the envelope in the attic. He told his wife that when he died, as his spirit ascended to Heaven, he would pick up the check so he could take his money with him. Several weeks after the man's death, his widow was carrying some things to store in the attic, and there on the floor she saw the envelope with the cashier's check inside. She smiled to herself, remembering his words about taking it with him when he ascended, and she said: "I knew he should have left it in the basement!" It is not money that makes life livable. Money is no more than a paper symbol, reminding us of what we can do or choose not to do to make the world a better place. But it cannot be taken with us.

It is the same with prestige and power. Mother Theresa had prestige; so did Jesse James. Albert Schweitzer had prestige; so did Idi Amin.

Jesus said that what matters most is not always what we give our time and efforts to. Instead, He said so very simply, here is what ultimately makes sense of life: *"You shall love the Lord your God...and you shall love your neighbor as yourself."* It's all about love. That divine truth is wise, honest, and simple.

Most of us realize that we tend to make life too complicated. Thus have I tried to develop a simple credo to live by. It is not exhaustive, and I really don't know whether it sounds more like Jesus or Robert Fulghum, but here is a simple list of things I try to keep in mind that helps me stay afloat amid the flood waters of life. My list of truths to live by:

– Love is stronger than hate.
– Faith is better than fear.

– Smiles and tears are both important, and we should be embarrassed by neither.

– Grief hurts. Don't deny it.

– Most people are better than we give them credit for being.

– Having a large balance in your bank account is not as meaningful as having people who want to go to lunch with you tomorrow or people who want you to come home in the afternoon.

– If you don't allow yourself productive quiet times, you'll never have much of worth to say when it's time for a conversation.

– Not everyone will like you. Get over it.

– Children are as close to being angels as anything we are ever going to see on this earth.

– If you make the decision to do one good deed every day, you will make the earth a different place.

– If you cannot say "I love you," you are missing a source of deep joy.

– If you cannot show love, you are missing the meaning of life.

That list of random thoughts is my personal formula for what makes sense of life. Its fabric is woven with a word that is divinely clear and comprehensible. "What is life all about?," He was asked. And Jesus answered: *"You shall love the Lord your God...and you shall love your neighbor as yourself."* It really is that simple.

Study or Discussion Questions

(1) Define your understanding of the word "Agape."

(2) Jesus said, *"You shall love your neighbor as yourself."* How, within the parameters of Christian discipleship, should one practice self-love?

(3) Discuss or consider the meaning of the words from the epistle of *John: "You cannot love God, whom you have not seen, if you hate your brother or sister, whom you have seen."*

(4) Name specific ways of putting love into action for people who are difficult to love.

(5) Write your own personal *credo* for life.

SMALL ACTS CAN BRING GREAT RESULTS

Read *John 13: 1-17*

There was a con artist named Arthur. His friends called him "Artie." He spent most of his time trying to bum people out of money for drinks. One day he went into a super market. On one aisle he met a man whom he asked for a dollar. The man refused, whereupon Artie got angry and tried to choke him. When the man fought back, Artie went to the next aisle where he spotted a woman. The same thing happened. He asked for a dollar. She refused, so he tried to choke her. About that time the police arrived and arrested him. The next day there was a headline in the local paper that said: "Artie chokes two for a dollar at Winn Dixie."

Obviously there are two ways of interpreting that headline—either "Artichokes two for $1" *or* "Artie chokes two for $1."

There are two ways of looking at lots of things. A date can be a day on the calendar or someone you're taking to movies. A dessert can be one's reward for good or evil (as in "getting their just desserts"), or it may be that which tops off a good meal; of course, for some it is the main course. (As the old saying puts it: "Life is tentative; eat dessert first!")

There are often two ways of looking at a scripture passage. Most folks read the Upper Room lesson from the gospel of *John* and focus on what Christ gives to us. We focus on the institution of what later became known as *The Lord's Supper*—how Jesus blessed bread and wine, pointed to his upcoming crucifixion on our behalf, and said: *"This do in remembrance of me."*

However, there is another way of looking at what happened that evening, and apparently that is how the author of John saw it. He tells the story from a different perspective than Matthew or Luke. John only refers to The Lord's Supper in one brief passing phrase. All he says about is: *"After supper had ended...."* That's it. That is all he says about the meal. However, John goes on then and devotes the rest of the lesson to something else Jesus did that night. It is not something ordinarily considered noble or sacramental, rather just a small act of courtesy. The disciples had walked the dusty roads coming into Jerusalem to reach that upper room, and the story says:

"Jesus took a towel...After that, He poured water into a basin and began to wash the disciples' feet...."

That seemed like such a little deed contrasted to something like Holy Communion, and yet apparently that is what the disciples remembered and talked about. That is how John got the story. He listened to the accounts of disciples when they discussed what occurred in the upper room. And apparently they were most impressed by a small act of courtesy which reflected the great Spirit of Christ.

Maybe, as odd as it sounds in our "bigger-is-better" world, sometimes it is a sacred moment when we dare to dream small. That is not to say that we settle for accomplishing only that which is insignificant. It is rather to say that we do not denigrate the value of little deeds that reveal great spirits.

Often when we do our religious remembering, we tend to concentrate on the heavyweights (Augustine, Calvin, Luther, Wesley, Asbury, or one of the celebrated papal leaders). That is legitimate because those folks and their contributions have helped shape the course of Christian history. But, there is another way of looking at church history, as well. At the end of the day, most of us have been shaped and influenced more dramatically by anonymous apostles: by a pastor or Sunday School teacher from your childhood…by some friend in the dorm or little league coach who cared about you and listened and prayed…by a grandmother who took you to summer revivals in her little country church, and then carried you back to her house for homemade lemonade and lots of love…by a Bible Study teacher who opened up the scriptures to you in a new and transforming way…by a friend at church who held your hand, stood beside you and gave you the strength to survive when alone you did not have that strength. Jesus *"took a towel…poured water into a basin and began to wash the disciples' feet."*

As a pastor, one of the things I do first when planning a funeral service is to sit with the family and ask them to talk about the deceased, to tell me stories, to help me to put together an accurate profile for the meditation. It never ceases to impress me what spouses and children choose to remember. I rarely hear about dad's winning the Congressional Medal of Honor or mom's starring on Broadway (even if those things are true). Instead, more often I hear things like:

"I remember a dress I wanted. Mom said we couldn't afford it, but when I didn't get chosen to be a cheerleader, and she knew how disappointed I was, that dress showed up in my closet. She was always doing things like that."

"I remember how Dad always fixed pancakes on Saturday mornings, and how he pretended to be interested in my cartoons on TV even when there was a ball game he really wanted to watch."

"I remember how Uncle Ted sat up with me half the night when my grandpa died. And he told me it was okay to cry. Almost all the others were so busy and broken that they didn't have time for a little boy like me. But Uncle Ted took time and cared."

Those are the stories pastors hear. And they seem to be such little things, hardly worth mentioning, one would think. They are such *small* acts of kindness and courtesy, not unlike the small act of thoughtfulness displayed by One who took a towel and a basin and washed his disciples' weary feet. And yet, it is often those very "little things" that we remember most, for frequently small things reflect great spirits.

An old poem speaks not of salvation, but rather of discipleship:

"Heaven's not gained in a single bound,
But by little things piled round on round."

Probably most of us will never win a Nobel Peace Prize. Perhaps we will never discover a vaccine for AIDS or write a book that brings about nuclear disarmament. Probably I will never preach a sermon that puts an end to racism, sexism or ageism. We may not be able to accomplish everything, but all of us can do something, even if it seems small, to make the world a better place. We were not put on this earth to take. We were created and placed here to give. The defining question of life should never be, "What's in it for me?" Instead, the one single question that will ultimately bring meaning to is this, "How can I be in it for others?" In time, most of us figure out that we cannot accomplish all things, but we can do something to make the world a better place.

Maybe we cannot feed all the world's hungry people, but we can support local agencies that put sandwiches in few outstretched hands. Maybe we cannot clothe all the world's naked people, but we can clean out our closets periodically and help a few. Maybe we cannot comfort every person who suffers, but almost every single day we can at least dry somebody's tears. Maybe we cannot save everyone's soul, but we can tell someone about Jesus or invite someone to church.

"Heaven's not gained in a single bound,
But by little things piled round on round."

In the first church I served after seminary was a woman named Sally. Sally was over ninety years old and home-bound. Due to age and arthritis, she could barely even move around in her own house. She had outlived most of her friends and the people with whom she had grown up. She spent her time alone in a little white frame house at the end of the road not far from the church. I remember receiving a call one day that Sally had died, and we needed to plan a funeral. I did not expect many folks to attend a memorial service for an aged widow who was a shut-in. But to my surprise, on the day of the service the church was full, and people were standing in the narthex and outside on the grass. Why? It was because every day Sally would sit down with the newspaper. She would read accident reports and the obituaries. And she would send a hand-written note to every accident victim who was injured and every family that was bereaved—a hand-written note expressing her love to strangers who suffered, and promising to them her prayers. It was such a little thing, just noticing other people who hurt and reminding them with a note that they did not hurt alone. But when Sally died, people who had never even met her came out by the hundreds to express thanks for someone who had cared about them in their darkest hours and by caring had helped to turn the lights back on. Sally never made the headlines. She never received any awards. But she had a sense of joy in her life, a sense of purpose and meaning, because every day she did something to make life better for somebody else.

So,

Go on writing those notes.

Go on phoning shut-ins or taking casseroles to homes where death has struck.

Go on seeking out visitors at church to make them feel welcome and wanted.

Go on tossing a frisbee with a child down the street whose daddy never comes around.

Go on teaching children to sing "Jesus Loves Me" or to quote the *Twenty-third Psalm*.

Go on helping and loving and listening to a friend at school or a co-worker on the job.

Those are "little things," of course, hardly noticeable at all (except to the person on the receiving end and, of course, to God). But by remaining faithful in just such little things, we join hands and hearts with a Savior who took a towel and a basin and washed his disciples' weary feet. And when He rose from that seemingly small task, he said: *"I have given you this example, that you should do (even) as I have done."*

FACET FIVE: *CORPORATE DISCIPLESHIP*

FACING FUNDAMENTALISM

Read *Mark 12: 28-34*

Recently one of my staff members gave me a list of suggested bumper sticker mottos that all fifty states might want to adopt. Consider just a select few, all of them tongue-in-cheek:

Maryland: If You Can Dream It, We Can Tax It
Arizona: Hey! It' Dry Heat
Delaware: We Like Chemicals In Our Water
Oregon: Spotted Owl - It Tastes Like Chicken
Michigan: Your First Line Of Defense Against Canadian Invasion

And, from a state I will leave unnamed in case a reader came from there, was the suggested motto: *We Put The "Fun" Back Into Fundamentalist Extremism*. Were it not too often true, it would be hilarious. We Put The "Fun" Back Into Fundamentalist Extremism.

There is, has always been, and, one suspects, will always be a debate regarding religious fundamentalism, and it is anything but "fun." It doesn't really matter whether you are Christian, Jewish or Muslim. The debate seems to rage within all of the world great religious communities.

As Christians, we know what the debate feels like in our own camp. There are *"litmus test questions"*......

Do you believe in the literal interpretation of *the Bible*?

Do you believe in the literal interpretation of the Virgin Birth?

Do you believe in the literal reality of hell?

Do you believe that *Revelation* is prophetic as opposed to apocalyptic?

And if you don't, then some will say you are not "fundamentally" a Christian. The debate rages on between those who view the Bible as "literal" and those who view it as "inspired," between those who see Christianity as a system of dogmatics and those who see it as a journey of faith and discipleship.

When Jesus was questioned about what it fundamentally means to be a believer, he didn't talk much about some of the issues we think are front and center. Instead, He talked about love. That's it. He said that fundamentally our faith is all about loving—believing that God loves us, and then doing our best to love God and one another. When it all boils down to fundamentals, Jesus said it all boils down to love.

There is a story about a love note a girl found taped to her locker at school? It was from her new boyfriend. She and he had just planned a date for Sunday. Something of an underachiever, he had no car or income but was going to walk to her house and bring a movie for the VCR. So, taped to her locker was this passionate note:

"For you I would cross the hottest desert. For you I would swim the deepest sea. For you I would climb the highest mountain. I love you. I love you. I love you. P.S. I'll see you Sunday if it doesn't rain!"

He proclaimed the principles of romance but missed the fundamentals.

Jesus was condemned by fundamentalists who missed the fundamentals. The Pharisees were always uptight about rules and regulations. They condemned Jesus (finally even to a Cross) because he didn't share their kind of fundamentalism. (1) They said they had fulfilled their obligation to God by paying their tithe (which is a wonderful thing, and every pastor would love to have a few more people who follow that example) but Jesus said that at the same time they were letting their aged parents go hungry. (2) They said that The Law was so paramount that anyone who broke it should be stoned—but Jesus believed in grace, fresh starts and second chances, and so he said to the woman they were about to kill: *"Your sins are forgiven; go your way, and sin no more."* (3) They believed it is wrong to work on the Sabbath—but Jesus placed people above ritual, healed the paralytic on the Sabbath, and, of course, the Pharisees condemned him for it.

The Pharisees were so bound by rules that there was no room for love, so committed to a strict interpretation of all the "Thou shalts" and "Thou shalt nots" that grace, compassion and charity were foreign concepts to them. The Pharisees were religious fundamentalists whose extremism made them almost sacrilegious. But the

Messiah, said: "If you want to talk fundamentals, it all boils down to love."

"One of the scribes came and heard them arguing, and recognizing that He had answered them well, asked him, 'What commandment is the foremost of all?' Jesus answered, 'The foremost is, Hear, O Israel! The Lord our God is one Lord. And you shall love the Lord your God with all your heart, and with all your soul, and with all your mind, and with all your strength. The second is this, You shall love your neighbor as yourself. There is no other commandment greater than these.'" Do we want to talk fundamentalism? Well, there we have it. According to Jesus, fundamentally it all boils down to love.

Someone shared with me a story he attributed to a woman named LaVonn Steiner. She told of her daddy's hardware store in Mott, North Dakota, a small town on the prairies. One year just before Christmas, she was helping out in her father's store when a little boy came in, no more than five or six years old. He was wearing a brown tattered coat with dirty, worn cuffs. She said his hair was scraggly, except for a Dennis the Menace cowlick at the crown of his head. His shoes were scuffed, and only one even had a lace in it. The child was obviously poor. In fact, from the looks of him, he was very poor. He browsed around the small toy section of the family hardware store, picked up items, examined them, and then very carefully put them back on the shelf. Ms. Steiner said her dad walked over to the child, as he would to any other customer, and asked if he could help. The little boy said, "I'm looking for a gift for my brother." Her dad told him to make himself at home. After about twenty minutes, the child picked up a carved toy airplane. He cradled it in his hands, as it if were made of crystal and carried to LaVonn's father. "How much is this?" he asked. "My brother loves planes."

Her dad answered: "How much do you have?"

The little boy reached into his tattered coat and pulled out a handful of change. He spread his money on the counter and began to count. "I have twenty-seven cents," he announced.

Her dad picked up the coins, smiled and said, "Isn't that something? That plane costs exactly twenty-seven cents!" He then put it in a box and wrapped it with paper and bow, and the child went out with a grin of total satisfaction. LaVonn went back to the toy section and found the plane's shipping box under the counter. Checking the price, she saw that it sold for $11.98. She never mentioned it to her father, nor did he say anything more about it to her, but she said: "My best gift that Christmas was seeing my dad's love in action!"

I don't know what church LaVonn Steiner's dad belongs to…or if he belongs to one at all…but I do know that what she saw him do that cold December day in North Dakota was fundamentally Christian. Love in action. That's what Jesus called believers to do when all the fine points of theology have been argued over and put away. *"What is the great commandment?,"* asked the scribe, and Jesus answered: *"You shall love the Lord your God…and you shall love your neighbor as yourself."* That is the New Testament definition of "fundamentalism," and it's a definition most compassionate and thinking believers can embrace and live with. We, as people of faith, are called upon purely and simply to love!

Take it one step further. Jesus encouraged his followers to: *"Love your enemies, and pray for those who despitefully use you."* Authentic Christian fundamentalism calls us to love people who are not easy to love…people who don't have the money to pay for the toy plane…people who disappoint us or abuse us or refuse to love us even when we try to love them. Christ-like love, which the Bible calls *"agape,"* is unconditional. We love imperfect people who don't deserve it because God loves us in our own imperfection. W.H. Auden captured the meaning of unconditional love with is words:

O stand, stand in the window
As the tears scald and start.
You shall love your crooked neighbor
With all your crooked heart.

Sam Keen has written a wonderful book entitled *To Love And Be Loved.* In it he talks about Christian *agape.* He says: "*Agape*…is the capacity to love worthless people…(to simply say) You exist, therefore you are worthy of loving!"

Christian fundamentalism does not give you and me the opportunity to choose whom we shall love and whom we shall hate, whom we shall nurture and whom we shall turn away. Christian fundamentalism simply says: For better or worse, "You exist, therefore you are worthy of loving!"

That is what "fundamentalism" means in the best and purest sense of the word. Biblically, it all boils down to love—love for God and love for people, sometimes even when people don't make loving easy.

In the Ken Burns' PBS series *The Civil War*, there were a number of scenes of the fiftieth anniversary of the Battle of Gettysburg in 1913. A group of old Confederate and Union veterans returned to commemorate the occasion.

Some rare films show the men talking over old times, sharing stories and eating together. Then there was a re-enactment of Pickett's Charge. The old Union soldiers took their places, as they had years earlier, among the rocks on Seminary Ridge. The old Confederate soldiers took their places on the farmland below. After a while, the Confederate soldiers started to move forward across the broad, flat field where just fifty years earlier so many had died. "We could not see rifles and bayonets," an eyewitness said, "but instead canes and crutches" as the old men made their slow advance toward the ridge. When the Confederate veterans got near the Union line, they broke into a long rebel yell. Then the most fascinating thing happened. Unable to restrain themselves any longer, the Union troops burst out from behind the stone wall and flung themselves upon their former enemies. Only this time, the men in gray and the men in blue didn't fight. Instead, the old men threw their arms around one another and stood and held on and wept. What a difference fifty years had made. In that moment they understood that we are created not to do battle with one another, but simply to love.

What is the bottom line for people of faith? What is Christianity fundamentally about? When all the debates and arguments are over, it all boils down to this: *"You shall love the Lord your God with all your heart, and all your mind, and all your soul, and all your strength. And you shall love your neighbor as yourself."*

Study or Discussion Questions

(1) Discuss or consider the differences between religious "fundamentalism" and religious "orthodoxy."

(2) The argument has been made that Jesus offended the religious hierarchy of his day because he called for a return to fundamental Hebraic faith and practice.

To what extent do you agree or disagree with that statement?

If there is validity to it, in what were the fundamentals that Jesus seemed to consider non-negotiable?

(3) List three "fundamental" principles of the Christian faith that you think are reasonably expected of all believers.

A

B

C

(4) Consider national or global examples of:

(A) Fundamental religious commitments that have helped enhance human life.

(B) Religious extremism that diminishes human life.

(5) What are the bottom-line fundamentals of faith to which you are committed?

A CHURCH WITHOUT PETTINESS

Read *Philippians 4: 1-9*

It is hard to describe what the internet has done to preaching. Since my sermons began appearing on line, I have received letters from people in Mississippi saying, "Let me tell you how the story you told really went. I'm the woman's minister," or from Ohio saying, "Thanks for saying all those nice things about me in your sermon last week." I pick up a story somewhere (I read it in the paper or hear someone tell it) and due to the internet, as soon as I preach it someone contacts me with editorial comments, thanks or critiques.

Such is my disclaimer to anyone in Tacoma, Washington, who may read this. The man who told me this story said "I *think* it happened in Tacoma, but I'm not sure." Anyway, there was a meeting of a local civic club a year ago out in Tacoma—or somewhere in the far

West—and they were debating how to spend the proceeds of their annual fund-raising event. There was a definite split opinion between those who wanted to give the money to their local charitable projects and those who wanted to use the money to help in renovations to the club's building. The debate that night was long, and as the evening wore on, rather heated. Voices were raised. Fingers were pointed. And friends who had worked side by side on the fund-raiser began to argue rather unkindly with one another. While the debate rolled on, two men entered the back room of the building unnoticed and walked away with every penny of the $8500 the civic club had raised. While they argued among themselves, they lost their shirts!

That often happens to groups or organizations when conflict overcomes compassion, when an individual's need to win is given priority over the organization's need to succeed. I often refer to the Philippian church because that was the primary New Testament model of what a church is meant to be. But, even there it was not Utopia. Paul was frightened that conflict and competition within that congregation could cripple the church in Philippi.

Apparently a feud was breaking out. There is an old adage: "When churches fight, the devil takes a vacation." Paul wanted to make sure that did not happen there. Two women who had worked side-by-side with him in getting the Philippian Church off the ground had a disagreement. Rather than forgiving, they fought. We do not know what the argument was about, but we do know that it was having a negative effect on the whole church. People were taking sides. A rift was forming. So Paul wrote to the leaders of the congregation and said: *"I plead with Euodia and I plead with Syntyche to agree with each other in the Lord. Yes, and I ask you, loyal friends, help these women who have contended at my side in the cause of the gospel...."*

Paul was telling those two women that no personal issue or agenda is important enough to let it threaten the health of a church, which he described as *"the Body of Christ."* He was also telling the members of the church to step in, to say "No" to conflict and become peacemakers, lest the devil get to take a vacation in Philippi.

How many local congregations urgently need to hear Paul's advice? Some churches are even known as "contentious," which is pretty much the opposite of being Christian. Upon investigation, churches like that rarely argue about anything worthy of the effort—things that would matter to Christ: evangelism, feeding the hungry, challenging systems that oppress the poor, inclusivity, etc. Those issues are worth our passions. But we all know congregations that became embroiled in controversy about issues like the color of the parlor carpet or landscaping or cemetery plots, issues which are in all likelihood of no interest to Christ whatsoever.

A church in a growing Southern town split into two congregations during a building program. They were putting up a new sanctuary in which to worship God. Everyone agreed on the desire and need for the sanctuary. That was not an issue. But one group wanted it to face the road to the north of the church property while the other wanted it to face the road to the south of the property. So, an argument ensued, and they split and built two churches...one facing north, and one facing south. Today each little church struggles just to stay alive, within half a mile of one another, whereas one strong church could have made an impact on that whole area of the city.

Every thinking person knows what church fights are usually about. They are rarely about the issues we claim. Instead, they are almost always about ego—about power, control and the hunger for it. Apparently both Euodia and Syntyche wanted their way in the church at Philippi.

An article in *U.S. Catholic Magazine* quoted Maxwell Perkins, the famous book editor. He said: "One of my deepest convictions is that the terrible harms that are done in this world are not done by deliberately evil people...They are done by basically good people, by those who are so sure that God is with them. Nothing can stop them, for they are certain that they are right." His words made me remember other words spoken by the wonderful Christian ethicist, the late Dr. George Kelsey. I heard him speak them years ago in a class at Drew University. He said: "Some of the most heinous acts ever committed were done by people who thought that God was on their side!"

In all likelihood Eudoia and Syntyche were good people who believed in their hearts that God was on their side and thus staked themselves out on some position. But good people are just as prone as anyone else to be more influenced by ego than by faith, grasped by the need for power, control and authority. Because of those two basically good people whose egos had gotten out of control, the devil was about to get a vacation in Philippi. So Paul went on and said to them: *"Let your gentleness be known to all...and the peace of God which passes all understanding will guard your hearts and minds in Christ Jesus."*

"Gentleness" is not always the standard we apply toward others with whom we have disagreements, despite the fact that Jesus taught, *"Do unto others as you would have them do unto you."* When arguments and conflicts arise, gentility frequently falls with Eutychus out the window. We hold the other person to tough standards, far tougher than we wish to be held to ourselves. We want to go for the jugular with them though we want them to extend grace to us.

A wonderful story is told about French novelist and playwright Alexandre Dumas. Though it certainly sounds apocryphal, the story goes that Dumas once had a heated quarrel with a rising young politician. The argument became so intense that a duel was inevitable. Each man was given a pistol containing one bullet. Since both men were superb shots they decided to draw lots, the loser agreeing to shoot himself. Dumas lost. Pistol in hand, he withdrew in silent dignity to another room, closing the door behind him. The rest of the company waited in gloomy suspense for the shot that would end his life. It rang out at last. His friends ran to the door, opened it, and found Dumas sitting there, very much alive, smoking revolver in hand. "Gentlemen, a most regrettable thing has happened," he announced. "I missed." Logic suggests that he would not have missed had he shot at his opponent.

When Paul wrote to the *Philippians* about *"the peace of God which passes all understanding,"* he quite literally was talking about not pulling the trigger even when we are tempted to. We frequently quote that text when people face hardship or tragedy with unusual confidence and calm. We say they possess a *"peace that passes understanding."* We clergy quote it that way all the time. But literally translated, Paul set this verse in the context of discord within the church. The church, he knew, is made up of people. And we people are imperfect and can therefore be selfish and petty. Paul called us to rise above all that for the sake of Christ and thus to love our neighbors, even when our neighbors are hard to love. Then we find *"the peace of God which passes understanding"*—a way to make peace when the logical, human tendency is to fume or fight.

How do we do that? We are, after all, humans. We do have clay feet. We do get feelings hurt and noses out of joint. So, how do we overcome all that and actually deal lovingly and peacefully with the other members of *"the Body of Christ?"*

Here is what Paul suggested: *"Whatever is true, whatever is noble, whatever is right, whatever is pure, whatever is lovely, whatever is admirable…think about those things."*

He told Euodia and Syntyche and any who were tempted to take sides with them, to re-focus. Focus on the faith, the goodness and the beauties of God and ministry within his fellowship. Paul was saying that the church is no place for pettiness—no place for a win-lose mindset—no place to say "If I don't get my way, I'll take my ball and go home."

"Remember why we built this church in Philippi," he said, and *"think about those things."*

In a world with *"wars and rumors of wars,"* I found it sobering and inspiring some time ago to hear a former astronaut reflect in a television interview about his journey into space. He talked of how it looked to peer down on the shining blue ball which we call "Earth," he said: "When you look down from that perspective, you realize it is all one small neighborhood in a vast Universe. We who live upon the planet are all neighbors with one another. And thus war and hatred become unthinkable. We are all called to keep the neighborhood clean and peaceful."

So it is with planet Earth...and so it is, as well, with The Christian Church. We are a family of faith, one small neighborhood of believers in a vast Universe of heartache and sin. Thus, Paul told those people in Philippi that war and hatred within *"the Body of Christ"* is unthinkable. We are called to keep our neighborhood clean, peaceful and loving. If the world is ever to learn what love and grace look like, it will only happen if they see it in us. And if we fail, then we have failed to answer our primary calling.

To be a church worthy of the name, Paul indicated, our focus must always be on that which is *"noble, pure, lovely and admirable."* Focus, he said, *"on those things."*

When Jesus set out to describe what Christians look like, he said: *"Blessed are the peacemakers."* It was a word of challenge for believers in the world *and* in the church.

Study or Discussion Questions

(1) What things should my church do to promote peace rather than disunity?

(2) How may I personally help make that happen?

(3) Discuss or consider the role of the ego in most church conflicts.

(4) when a church conflict exists, what are the best practical methods for resolving it?

(5) Discuss or consider the practice of triangulation (going to a third party in times of conflicts as opposed to going to the person with whom one has an issue) and the importance of honest but compassionate conversation.

AN I-CENTERED CHURCH

Read *Matthew 28: 16-20; I Corinthians 9: 16-23*

A little boy was told to say his bed-time prayers, while mama and daddy stood by and watched. They were filled with pride when reverently he knelt beside his bed, bowed his head and folded his hands. But the sweet ambiance ended when they heard him say:

"God take care of me and my friends.
Just see that we are blest.
And once You've taken care of us,
The devil can have the rest."

To write of the importance of being "An I-Centered Church" sounds about that small and self-absorbed. However, in this case that phrase is simply a literary device to address what *The Great Commission* calls churches to do and be.

In a meeting of the Mission and Ministry Committee, people began to suggest words that they felt described activities which should be at the center of what "church" means. I quickly took out a mustard-stained paper napkin from my coat pocket and began to write those words down. The four on which we focused that night, oddly enough, all began with the letter "I." It was there that I began to understand a bit of the biblical beauty of being "An I-Centered Church."

(1) The first word I wrote down was **INVITE**.

It turned out to be a singularly important word because a decision was made that night to make it the central operative word for the next two years in the life of our church. Those involved in the decision all felt that any church worth the title *Christian* is by definition called to be warm, welcoming and invitational.

Imagine yourself in the military, boarding a plane to the Iraq. Your spouse and children are standing close in tears, saying "good-bye." You are unsure if you will ever see them again in this world. What would you say to people whom you love more than life itself? You would not waste that final moment talking about sports, laundry or re-roofing the house. Rather, you would tell them you love them, or you will pray for them. You would want your final words to be the most important thing possible to say.

When Jesus was about to ascend into Heaven, he stood for the final time with his disciples—the people whom he loved like family. He had to determine the one last word he wanted to share with them, the one final message he hoped they would not forget. And what did He say?

"Go into all the world, making disciples."

The final word, the lasting message, of the Savior

himself had to do with invitation, evangelism and inclusivity—with reaching out beyond the walls of the church and bringing others in. If it were that important to Him, how can it be anything less than crucial to us?

Sixty percent of Americans are functionally unchurched. Half of those people say they do not attend church because no one has ever invited them to any church at any time. If such is the case, then we may well have failed to take seriously the final words of Jesus.

(2) The second word inscribed on my mustard-stained napkin was **INVOLVE**.

There is a place at God's table for everyone. Everyone. In Paul's letter to the *Corinthians,* he spoke of a church made up of *"slaves and free," "Jews and Gentiles," "those who live by the Law and those who are weak."* In short, Paul was telling the church in Corinth that *all people* are valued—and wanted—and needed. They all had something of worth to give, and the church needed those unique gifts.

It is the same in any congregation. When you enter your church, you bring skills, talents and dreams with you. And there is a place for you and all your unique gifts at the table. To simply sit in a sanctuary for an hour a week makes you part of the *congregation.* But when you become involved in a Bible study group—or a Sunday School class—or a choir—or some task force that's service-oriented, then you become part of the *fellowship.* When you bring your talents to some specific area of the life of the church, the church becomes stronger and you no longer feel like a stranger there, but rather like part of the family.

Studies by religious sociologists consistently reveal the same conclusion. Survey after survey indicates that people desire to be part of a congregation where they can live out their discipleship, where they are given opportunities to practice what is preached. It is not enough merely to INVITE people to this sacred place; church truly matters when we are INVOLVED.

(3) A third word we discussed that night was **INSTRUCT**.

In *The Great Commission* Jesus told the disciples to *"Go into all the world making disciples, baptizing them in the name of the Father, the Son and the Holy Spirit, and teaching them…."*

There was an aged woman in one of my early churches who always came to worship and Church Night suppers, but never set foot in a Sunday School class. She had been very active in a class for years, and once was even its President, but about age sixty she just quit. For twenty years afterward, no matter how much her friends asked her to come back, she refused. This is what she would tell them: "I already know more than I'm willing to act on!" Humorous, yes, but the fact is that she was probably serious. "I already know more than I'm willing to act on!"

Jesus would have taken issue with that. So should we all. As parents, spouses, professional people or Christians, we never know enough. As a seminarian it seemed odd to me to see a number of retired professors who every day would make a pilgrimage to the library. There you would find them in the stacks, bending over old theological volumes, taking notes as if they themselves were students. Back then I wondered why anyone would do that if they didn't have to. Now I wonder why anyone would ever stop doing it. It is the journey of the mind that keeps us young. God has countless undiscovered treasures for those who keep searching.

Among the most important things we do in church are such activities as Sunday School and Vacation Bible School, small group Bible study or theological exploration, or any other forums where we open ourselves to God's wisdom which makes life exciting—and which keep our spirits young.

(4) The final word discussed that night was **INSPIRE**.

In the passage to the *Corinthians*, Paul was inspired. He was literally "on fire" to be about God's business. He wrote: *"I am compelled to preach. Woe unto me if I preach not the gospel!"* He had a story to share, and he could not rest till he shared it.

There was an Army private in a camp in Kansas who had a girlfriend in Oklahoma. Every Friday he asked for a weekend pass so he could go see her. And every week the Commanding Officer gave the pass to somebody else. Finally, after everyone in his barracks had been given a pass, he knew it was his turn. But instead, the C.O. gave it to someone to whom it had been awarded before. With that, the straw broke the camel's back. So that night, the soldier hopped in a jeep and drove toward the main gate. The guard on duty shouted "Halt!," but the young private kept coming. The guard leveled his rifle at the jeep and once more shouted "Halt!" This time the driver yelled back: "I have a mama in Heaven, a daddy in hell and a girlfriend in Oklahoma. And I plan to see one of them tonight!" The man was on a mission. He was inspired.

We should be, too. Christians have the greatest message on earth. We have been given a secret that can end hostility between individuals and nations…that can bring confidence to those who are afraid…and hope to those who are discouraged…and peace to those who are troubled…and love to those who feel unspeakably alone. Believers know what a difference Jesus Christ can make in a human life. And that should inspire us, sometimes through words of faith or other times through deeds of courage or kindness, to share that good news with others. How can we know His power, comfort and love and not pass it along to others who struggle and suffer? As Paul said, *"I am compelled to preach. Woe unto me if I preach not the gospel!"*

In a Mission and Ministry Committee, I eavesdropped as church members talked and jotted down on a napkin their vision of "An I-Centered Church." It is a vision of a church that

INVITES, INVOLVES, INSTRUCTS and INSPIRES.

It's just what Jesus had in mind when he said: *"Go into all the world, making disciples of all people, baptizing them in the name of the Father, the Son and the Holy Spirit, and teaching them…*(And as you do it), *Lo! I will be with you, always…."*

Study or Discussion Questions

(1) What things should my/our church do to attract more first-time visitors to worship?

(2) How may I personally help make that happen?

(3) How can a church effectively help its members use their gifts and graces for ministry?

(4) Discuss or consider the role of Christian education in the overall life of a church.

(A) What does our church do to challenger the minds of persons?

(B) How is our church in any sense an "academy persence" in the community?

(C) How can our church partner with institutions of higher education to offer a stronger ministry to the congregation and the community at-large?

(D) What is the role of child care in the ministry of education?

(5) How does my church inspire persons to lives of Christian discipleship? What more might I do to help?

A CHURCH WORTH PRAISING

Read *Philipians 1: 1-11; 2: 19-30; 4: 14-19; Acts 16*

A woman went into the confessional booth at her local Roman Catholic church. Looking through the shutters, she saw the face of a man she didn't know. "Pardon me," she said, "but you are not Father O'Flannery. Are you a new priest I haven't met?"

The man answered, "No ma'am. I'm just in here to polish the woodwork."

"Well," the woman continued, "where is Father O'Flannery?"

The custodian whispered, "I'm not sure, lady. But judging from what some of his church members have said to me since I sat down in this box, I hope he's gone to get the police!"

I suppose most churches have a collection of sinners. Some are in the pews; others are in the pulpits. We just don't always confess it. But, as Paul said: *"All have sinned and fall short of the glory of God."*

The fable is told about what happened when God was creating animals to put on the earth. A group of angels saw Him at work and said: "That looks like fun." So, God allowed them to get together as a committee and told them they could create one animal. The angels could not agree on what kind of animal to create. Some liked one thing, some another. Eventually they compromised and created the platypus—an animal with the bill of a duck, the fur of an otter, the tail of a beaver and the feet of a frog. After that, God decreed that there would be no more committees in Heaven! Churches not only have sinners, they also have committees, which may well be worse.

It is easy to find fault with most congregations: for what they fail to do, or what they choose to do, or how they choose to do it. That is not a new thing. Read *Colossians, Ephesians, Corinthians,* the description of the seven churches in *Revelation,* or most any of the New Testament epistles. In those letters you will read of churches that tried the patience of the saints. But there is one that is different, almost pure and Christlike, a model of what a church is designed to be. Again we consider the Philippian church. It remains the New Testament's model of what true churches are meant to be. When Paul wrote to the church at Philippi, he said: *"I thank God in all my remembrance of you."* That is a mouthful. In spite of sinners, in spite of committees, in spite of human faults and frailties, there was something about the congregation in Philippi that made Paul pray a prayer of thanks every time he thought of them.

Paul, literally in love with the Philippian church,

wrote: *"For God is my witness, how I yearn for you all with the affection of Jesus Christ."*

(1) One of the things he appreciated most was that **THE PHILIPPIANS LOVED PAUL IN HIS TIMES OF LONELINESS AND DESPAIR.**

Paul referred to *"Epaphroditus…your messenger and minister to my needs."* Paul was in prison in Rome, doubtless feeling alone and afraid, but the people in Philippi did not settle for sending him Christmas cards or fruit baskets. They sent a man named Epaphroditus to stay there, to be with him in his suffering, to make sure he was being treated fairly, that he was healthy, and to remind him that he had not been forgotten.

A woman's husband committed suicide. She was understandably devastated, as were their children. But, she said every week another woman came from their little church in South Carolina, wearing a Stephen Ministry lapel pin. "Sometimes," she said, "she would sit and listen to me. Sometimes she would help with Thank-You notes. Sometimes she would clean the kitchen. Sometimes she would help my kids with their homework. And sometimes she would just put her arm around my shoulders while I cried. But every time she came, I knew my church was there and my God was there. Somehow because of that I survived."

Paul praised the Philippian church because it reached out to him in his dark and desperate moments. That is what Christlike churches do. He praised them for sending *"Epaphroditus…your messenger and minister to my needs."*

(2) Another reason Paul loved the church in Philippi was because **IT BELIEVED IN MISSIONAL MINISTRY.**

Here is how he put it: *"Even in Thessalonica you sent me help once and again."* Paul, throughout his ministry, labored to raise funds for the needy, especially for the young Christians in Jerusalem who were facing persecution and financial disaster. Unfortunately, not all the churches he established were overtly generous. But Philippi was. Many scholars feel that for the most part, the church people in Philippi were not particularly wealthy. Even so, they set aside money from their own paltry incomes to help others who had even less.

A devoted disciple of Christ named Dr. Joe Hale for many years he led The World Methodist Council, circling the globe countless times. He preached in the great shrines and cathedrals of the world. He also walked through jungles to preach in open air or beneath straw arbors. He probably knows more than anyone about Methodism's impact on every continent. I heard Dr. Hale say in a sermon some time ago that Methodism has survived and grown primarily because it does not stop with preaching; it also practices. He said that every time you find tragedy or need in this world, there you also find people called Methodists trying desperately to heal the hurts. Fill in the denominational blank—Lutheran, AME, CME, Presbyterian, Baptist, Roman Catholic, Episcopal, etc. The story will be the same. Christian churches do not stop with preaching; they also practice. One of the most inspiring witnesses in recent memory is what happened in the wake of Hurricane Katrina when churches of all denominations across America sent tens of millions of dollars to help and heal folks whom they would never meet nor know. More than preaching, persons of faith practiced what they profess to believe.

The people in Philippi never missed a chance to reach out to others in an effort to heal hurts. They were diligent in helping folks who could not help themselves. And that, as much as anything else, led Paul to say: *"I thank God in all my remembrance of you."*

(3) There is a third thing: **THE PHILIPPIAN CHURCH WAS EVANGELISTIC AND INCLUSIVE.**

Everyone was welcome there, and everyone was wanted. In the sixteenth chapter of *Acts* there is a description of the make-up of that church. It mentions a woman named Lydia, a wealthy, oriental merchant in whose house the congregation often met. It also mentions a jailer, a middle class citizen of Rome who lived and worked in Philippi. And then it mentions a local slave woman, a fortune teller who was a hometown girl, impoverished, and, until Paul got there, literally owned by some Philippian men. A rich foreign business woman…a middle class working Roman government official…and a local slave girl who was at the bottom of society's totem pole…and they were all welcome, wanted, and of equal importance in the Philippian church. It was a church with open doors, open arms and open hearts. It was a church that reached out with passion to invite others in, and loved them once they got there.

When my friend Bill Quick went to a large church in downtown Detroit, he was assigned to a great, historic building that was slowly becoming an empty showplace to a past when leading Detroit aristocracy kept the church alive and bursting at the seams. However, over the years the environment around it had changed. Most of the wealthy had moved away. Suburbs were now the centers of growth and commerce. The area around the church was in economic decline. People felt unsafe coming out for night meetings, as you could look out the windows on one side of the building and see the prostitutes and circling cars. You could look out the other side and see drug deals going down. All the nice folks who loved their church—and continued to drive in from the suburbs to worship there—were profoundly frightened. But then that new preacher, a southern boy from North Carolina, said to them: "We have two choices. We can build bigger fences and hide from our parish, or we can open our doors and evangelize it." To their everlasting credit, the people at that Detroit congregation chose option number two. They went out into the surrounding neighborhoods, out in the streets, and said to people: "We want you to be with us." In time, the old establishment in the pews began to say: "Our church is a rainbow." All colors, classes and backgrounds were wanted and welcome there. Someone who worshiped there not long ago told me: "That church is more alive than it's ever been. And Michael," she said, "you ought to see it. A sanctuary full of Whites, Blacks, Hispanics, Oriental-Americans...people in tailored clothes sharing hymnals with people who shop at Good Will...nurses seated next to hookers...businessmen next to street people...folks from mansions co-chairing committees with people from the projects. An old church in need of reviving has been resurrected because they opened their doors and hearts and invited people on the outside to come in.

There is a myriad of lessons to be learned from churches like that. Perhaps the primary lesson is that we all know people on the outside who should be invited in. It will make them better and stronger when they come. And it will make our congregations better and stronger, too. Herb Miller frequently reminded seminar attendees that every active church-goer knows an average of seven people who are not actively involved in church, four of whom would come next Sunday if we just invited them. That is the key to a church's future, if it truly wants one. People need your church. Likewise, your church needs them. And if we love our church, and if we love people, and if we love Christ, then not a week should pass that we do not invite someone to come and worship where we do.

The Philippians, probably more than any other New Testament congregation, were "a church worth praising." They were a model of what real churches ought to be. And the secret was simple.

In the name of Christ,

They loved lonely or frightened people.

They helped needy or hurting people.

and,

They invited and welcomed all people.

And because of that, Paul said: *"I thank God in all my remembrance of you."*

Study or Discussion Questions

(1) Discuss or consider how your church might become more inclusive.

(2) Discuss or consider how various socio-educational and ethnic groups add to the life of a single Christian community of believers.

(3) What basic discipleship commitments should any Christian congregation reasonable make?

(4) How can I individually help honor and achieve those commitments?

(5) Write a Mission Statement for:
– Your personal life as a Christian.
– The life of your congregation.

Printed in the United States
96038LV00001B/52-123/A